H. H. Walker

The Practice on Signing Judgment in the High Court of Justice

With Forms

H. H. Walker

The Practice on Signing Judgment in the High Court of Justice
With Forms

ISBN/EAN: 9783337159382

Printed in Europe, USA, Canada, Australia, Japan

Cover: Foto ©Suzi / pixelio.de

More available books at **www.hansebooks.com**

THE PRACTICE

ON SIGNING JUDGMENT

IN THE

HIGH COURT OF JUSTICE.

With Forms.

By H. H. WALKER,

JUDGMENT DEPARTMENT, EXCHEQUER DIVISION.

LONDON:
STEVENS AND SONS, 119, CHANCERY LANE,
Law Publishers and Booksellers.
1879.

TO

THE RIGHT HONOURABLE

SIR FITZROY KELLY,

LORD CHIEF BARON,

THIS WORK IS,

BY HIS PERMISSION,

AND

WITH PROFOUND RESPECT,

Dedicated

BY

HIS LORDSHIP'S MOST OBEDIENT SERVANT

THE AUTHOR.

PREFACE.

It is hoped that this little work may effect a saving of time and trouble, and be of mutual advantage to the Profession and the Officers of the Court. It professes merely to give all the information within the knowledge of the Author on points of every-day practice, and, in a condensed form, the answers to questions of every-day occurrence, together with such cases as have arisen and been decided under the Judicature Acts, in which the new practice differs from the old. The Author can only pretend to speak with accuracy of the practice of his own department; but he believes that, between the Common Law Divisions the divergencies are slight and unimportant, and that as the Chancery Division is governed by the same Rules, the practice cannot materially differ. He takes this opportunity of thanking his colleagues of the Queen's Bench and Common Pleas Divisions for the information they have been kind enough to give him.

January, 1879.

CONTENTS.

	PAGE
PREFACE	v

INTRODUCTION.

As to the Entry of Judgments generally	1

CHAPTER I.

Judgment for Non-appearance after Personal Service of Writ, Specially Indorsed According to Order 3, Rule 6, on Defendant, or some Person Authorized to be Served by the Rules . .	7

CHAPTER II.

Judgment for Non-appearance on Order for Substituted Service, when the Writ is Specially indorsed	26

CHAPTER III.

Judgment for Non-appearance where the Plaintiff's Claim is for a Liquidated Demand, but the Writ is not Specially Indorsed . . .	28

CHAPTER IV.

Judgment for Non-appearance when the Plaintiff's Claim is Unliquidated	30

CHAPTER V.

Judgment for Non-appearance for the Recovery of Land alone, or for the Recovery of Land and Mesne Profits, Arrears of Rent, or Damages for Breach of Contract	32

CHAPTER VI.

Judgment for Non-appearance under the Bills of Exchange Act	35

CHAPTER VII.

Judgment for Non-appearance where the Appearance is Struck Out or Set Aside by Order .	39

CONTENTS.

CHAPTER VIII.
Judgment under Order 14, Rule 1 . . . 40

CHAPTER IX.
Judgment for Want of Statement of Defence . 43

CHAPTER X.
Judgment for not Entering Demurrer for Argument 51

CHAPTER XI.
Judgment on Confession of Defence . . . 53

CHAPTER XII.
Judgment on Taking Money Out of Court . . 55

CHAPTER XIII.
Judgment on Judge's Order 58

CHAPTER XIV.
Judgment on Warrant of Attorney and Cognovit . 60

CHAPTER XV.
Judgment on Master's Certificate 62

CHAPTER XVI.
Judgment on Writ of Inquiry . . . 67

CHAPTER XVII.
Judgment on County Court Certificate . 68

CHAPTER XVIII.
Judgment on Award 70

CHAPTER XIX.
Judgment by Rule of Court, on Motion for Judgment, Demurrer and Special Case . . . 74

CHAPTER XX.
Judgment After Trial 79

CHAPTER XXI.
Judgment for Defendant 84

CHAPTER XXII.
New and Third Parties 86

CHAPTER XXIII.
The Attorneys' Act 97

CHAPTER XXIV.
Interpleader 98
FORMS 99
INDEX 133

INTRODUCTION.

---o---

AS TO THE ENTRY OF JUDGMENTS GENERALLY.

The following are the Rules particularly affecting the Entry of Judgment:—

Order 41.

Rule 1. Every judgment shall be entered by the proper officer in the book to be kept for the purpose. The party entering the judgment shall deliver to the officer a copy of the whole of the pleadings in the action other than any petition or summons; such copy shall be in print, except such parts (if any) of the pleadings as are by these Rules permitted to be written: Provided that no copy need be delivered of any pleading a copy of which has been delivered on entering any previous judgment in such action. The forms in Appendix (D) hereto may be used, with such variations as circumstances may require.

Rule 2. Where any judgment is pronounced by the Court or a Judge in Court, the entry of the judgment shall be dated as of the day on which such judgment is pronounced, and the judgment shall take effect from that date.

Rule 3. In all cases not within the last preceding Rule, the entry of judgment shall be dated as of the day on which the requisite documents are left with the proper officer for the purpose of such entry, and the judgment shall take effect from that date.

Rule 4. Where under the Act or these Rules, or otherwise, it is provided that any judgment may be entered or signed upon the filing of any affidavit or production of any document, the officer shall examine the affidavit or document produced, and if the same be regular and contain all that is by law required, he shall enter judgment accordingly.

Rule 5. Where by the Act or these Rules, or otherwise, any judgment may be entered pursuant to any order or certificate, or return to any writ, the production of such order or certificate sealed with the seal of the Court, or of such return, shall be a sufficient authority to the officer to enter judgment accordingly.

Rule 6. Any judgment of nonsuit, unless the Court or a Judge otherwise directs, shall have the same effect as a judgment upon the merits for the defendant; but in any case of mistake, surprise, or accident, any judgment of nonsuit may be set aside on such terms, as to payment of costs and otherwise, as to the Court or a Judge shall seem just.

Two copies of the judgment must be produced to the Officer: one to be filed, and one to be returned to the Solicitor. They must be exactly similar, and when printed forms are used, the form adapted to the case must be employed; alterations and erasures (except such as are unavoidable) cannot be allowed.

They must be of the proper size.

They may be written or printed.

The Letter and Number must be given in all cases, and when the writ was issued in a District Registry, and the cause has afterwards been removed to London, they must be the London letter and number.

Judgments cannot be amended except by order of the Court or a Judge, and the rule or order must be filed.

On signing judgment for Non-appearance, the Affidavit of personal service of the writ, or the Order for substituted service under the Judicature Acts, or Order to proceed under the Bills of Exchange Act, is filed in the judgment department. An affidavit of the service of the order and copy writ in the manner ordered must be filed with the order under the Judicature Acts, but under the Bills of Exchange Act no affidavit of the service of the order is required. A memorandum should be indorsed on the order and signed by the person serving it.

A Certificate of non-appearance must be produced on signing judgment in the Queen's Bench and Exchequer, not in the Common Pleas. The certificate must be dated the day it is to be used, and the search for appearance should be made immediately before signing judgment.

As to the Date of the judgment see Rules 2 and 3 preceding. Rule 2 applies to all judgments on Rule of Court and by direction of the Judge in Court at or after the Trial. Rule 3 to all other cases.

The Costs must, in all cases in which the judgment carries costs (except when it is for the recovery of land), be inserted in the judgment, or declared to be waived or paid, before execution can be issued.

The only cases in which a fixed amount is allowed for costs are judgments for Non-appearance after personal service of the writ on the defendant, or service in some mode prescribed by the rules, when £3 14s. is allowed in Town cases, and £4 6s. in Country and Agency cases, without taxation. Town cases are those in which the defendant's address is within three miles in a direct line from the General Post Office, all beyond are Country. There is also a fixed sum of £3 10s. for costs on judgment on Warrant of Attorney. In

Entry of Judgment.

all cases of personal service on a sole defendant who has not appeared, the fixed allowance must be taken at the time of signing judgment. The £4 6s. includes all charges for mileage, agency, &c., and the Masters will not tax under any circumstances.

When there are several defendants, 5s. will be allowed for each extra service, or the plaintiff may tax, at his option.

On an order for substituted service the plaintiff is entitled to tax, unless the order directs that no extra costs be allowed.

The Fee on signing judgment is 10s. in all cases, to be affixed to the copy filed in one adhesive stamp. There is also a fee of 2s. for filing the affidavit, but none for filing the order for substituted service, nor the pleadings when they are required to be filed.

In the Q. B. 6d. is charged for the solicitor's copy, but not in the C. P. or Exchequer.

An Office copy of the judgment which has the same force and effect as the original may be taken, on payment of a fee of 6d. per folio, and, when necessary, it may be certified to be a true copy by the Master.

The Certificate of the Master may also be obtained for the purpose of enforcing a judgment in Scotland and Ireland, under the Judgments Extension Act, 31 & 32 Vict. c. 54. The certificate and affidavit in support of it, under rule 5, must be brought to the judgment office to be examined; the affidavit is filed (fee, 2s.), and the certificate is then signed by the Master. The affidavit must be made by the solicitor applying for the certificate, who probably signed the judgment.

The fee on searching for Judgments is 2s. 6d.; for Affidavits, 1s.

Execution may be issued on the judgment immediately it is completed, and at any time within six years, unless a period for payment is mentioned in the judgment: Order 41, rule 15.

When six years have elapsed, or any change has taken place in the parties since the judgment was signed, an order must be obtained to be at liberty to issue execution: Order 41, rule 19.

CHAPTER I.

JUDGMENT FOR NON-APPEARANCE AFTER PERSONAL SERVICE OF WRIT, SPECIALLY INDORSED ACCORDING TO ORDER 3, RULE 6, ON DEFENDANT, OR SOME PERSON AUTHORIZED TO BE SERVED BY THE RULES.

This is the commonest and simplest form of Judgment for Non-appearance under the Judicature Acts; all that is necessary to enable the plaintiff to sign judgment for any sum not exceeding the sum indorsed on the writ is :—

1. That the Writ should be specially indorsed under Order 3, rule 6 ;
2. That it should have been personally served on the Defendant, and the day of the week and month of the service indorsed on the writ within three days after the service (Order 9, rules 2 and 13);
3. That the Affidavit of service should be in due form ;

Judgment for Non-Appearance.

(*a*) 4. That a Certificate of non-appearance, dated the day judgment is to be signed, and the writ, or a copy of it, should be produced.

As to the Indorsement on the Writ.

The words of Order 3, rule 6, are:—

"In all actions where the plaintiff seeks merely to recover a debt or liquidated demand in money payable by the defendant, with or without interest, arising upon a contract, express or implied, as, for instance, on a bill of exchange, promissory note, cheque, or other simple contract debt, or on a bond or contract under seal for payment of a liquidated amount of money, or on a statute where the sum sought to be recovered is a fixed sum of money or in the nature of a debt, or on a guaranty, whether under seal or not, where the claim against the principal is in respect of such debt or liquidated demand, bill, cheque, or note, or on a trust, the writ of summons may be specially indorsed with the particulars of the amount sought to be recovered, after giving credit for any payment or set-off."

And of Order 13, rule 3:—

"In case of non-appearance by the defendant, where the writ of summons is specially indorsed, under Order 3, Rule 6, the plaintiff may sign final judgment for any sum not exceeding the sum in-

(*a*) This is not required in the Common Pleas.

dorsed on the writ, together with interest at the rate specified, if any, to the date of the judgment, and a sum for costs, but it shall be lawful for the Court or a Judge to set aside or vary such judgment upon such terms as may seem just."

It follows, therefore, that, in order to be able to sign judgment under Order 13, rule 3, the writ must have been specially indorsed under Order 3, rule 6. In all cases in which this rule is not complied with, the proceedings must be under Order 13, rule 5.

Forms of indorsement under Order 3, rule 6, are given in the first schedule to the Act, Appendix A., section 7, but as they are preceded by a set of forms in section 2, although these are headed "money claims where NO special indorsement under Order 3, rule 6," they have been frequently adopted, under the erroneous impression that they were sufficient to entitle the plaintiff to immediate judgment, notwithstanding the plain contradiction in the heading.

From the words of Order 3, rule 6, and the Forms in section 7, it would seem that, in order to comply with these and entitle the plaintiff to final judgment for non-appearance, the indorsement on the writ, in all cases when the claim is for goods sold, or work done, and in all matters of account, should contain—

1. Dates and items.
2. Debits and credits.

"To goods" is a sufficient item, but comparing the words of the Rule, and of Form 1, section 7, it is doubtful whether "To balance due this day" is sufficient. The best way to determine what is, and what is not, a special indorsement, is by comparing section 2 and section 7 of the Appendix, the former of which gives a great many more examples of indorsements that are not special than the latter of those that are.

From a case already decided, *Walker* v. *Hicks*, L. R. 3 Q. B. D. 8, it appears that the forms in section 7 are to be followed in cases to which they apply, and should serve as models in others.

When Interest is claimed on the amount indorsed on the writ from the date of the writ until payment or judgment, the claim must be indorsed on the writ, otherwise judgment cannot be signed for it.

As to the Affidavit of Service (a).

Order 13, rule 2. Where any defendant fails to appear to a writ of summons, and the plaintiff is desirous of proceeding upon default of appearance under any of the following Rules of this Order, or under Order 15, Rule 1, he shall, before taking such proceeding upon default, file

---

(a) The whole of the dicta on the legal requirements of an affidavit are taken from Chitty's Practice and Day's Common Law Procedure Act; it has not, therefore, been considered necessary to cite the cases referred to by these unimpeachable authorities.

an affidavit of service, or of notice in lieu of service, as the case may be.

And by Order 41, rule 4, already cited, it is the duty of the Officer of the Court to see that the affidavit is regular, and contains all that is by law required.

The principal requisites are the following :—

Title.

The Affidavit should be intitled in the Court, but this may be shown on the face of it. It must be intitled in the Cause, the Christian and Surnames of all the parties must be stated at length, or as in the writ; " A. *v.* B. and others," is bad. The parties must be described as they are in the writ; " A. *v.* B. sued as, &c.," is bad. It must clearly appear who are Plaintiffs and who Defendants; " C. D. *ats.* A. B." is bad. Where the defendant is sued in a wrong name, he must be so described in the title of the affidavit. Where he is sued by an initial, the affidavit should be so intitled. Where parties sue, or are sued, in a representative capacity, it should appear in the title of the affidavit in what character they sue, or are sued, and of whom they are executors, administrators, assignees, &c. Exor., &c.; admor., &c.; assee., &c., are defective.

An affidavit with a defective title cannot be used even if the objection is waived.

Deponent's Address and Description.

"The addition and true place of abode of every person making an affidavit should be inserted therein." Regulæ Generales, 138, Hilary Term, 1853.

A defective address or addition to one of several deponents would render the affidavit inadmissible, and although the breach of this rule is only an irregularity which may be waived, it is not likely to be waived in an affidavit of service. "The above-named Plaintiff" (or Defendant) is a sufficient description of the deponent, without inserting the place of abode or any other addition; but "clerk to the Plaintiff," or to the "Plaintiff's Attorney," is not sufficient. The address must be the present one. A deponent cannot describe himself as "late of" one place, when he actually resides at another. The place of business of the deponent's employer is a sufficient address. "Of the City of London, merchant," "of Bath, in the County of Somerset, Esquire," are sufficient.

The rank or degree in life, profession, or trade of the deponent must be stated with sufficient certainty, unless he is a party in the cause; and it would seem that every person in the employ of another should state by whom he is employed. "Assessor," "acting as managing clerk," "articled clerk," are bad; but " late clerk to ——," " managing clerk to ——," " agent of the plaintiff," are good. " Merchant," " manufacturer," " process server," are sufficient.

The affidavit, if made in this country, must be signed by the deponent, but if he is described in the body as " John Thomas Smith," and signed " Thos. John Smith," this will do.

An affidavit re-sworn need not be re-signed.

It need not be signed in countries where it is not the custom.

Contents.

" Every affidavit to be hereafter used in any cause or civil proceeding in any of the Superior Courts of Common Law, shall be drawn up in the first person, and shall be divided into paragraphs, and every paragraph shall be numbered consecutively, and, as nearly as may be, shall be confined to a distinct portion of the subject." Regulæ Generales, 2, Mic. Vac. 1854.

The deponent must swear that he did, on the —— day of ——, personally serve the defendant with a true copy of the writ, and that he did, on —— the —— day of ——, indorse on the writ the day of the week and month of such service.

When the service is on some person other than the defendant, or in some mode authorised by the rules, the deponent must state facts, and not draw inferences; that is, in the case of a firm, under Order 9, rule 6, he should swear that he did personally serve ——, the manager, or ——, one of the partners of the firm, and not that he did serve the firm by leaving a copy writ with the manager or one of the partners. In the case of a public company, he should swear that he did personally serve the secretary, or post a letter addressed to the company, and not that he did serve the company by posting a letter, &c.

Order 9, rule 13: "The person serving a Writ of Summons shall, within three days at most after such service, indorse on the Writ the day of the month and week of the service thereof, otherwise the Plaintiff shall not be at liberty, in case of non-appearance, to proceed by default; and every affidavit of service of such writ shall mention the day on which such indorsement was made."

The writ cannot be served on a Sunday. Such service is void by statute 29 Car. II. There is no rule to prevent the indorsement being made on a Sunday, unless it may be inferred from Order 57, rule 2.

"When any limited time less than six days from or after any date or event is appointed or allowed for doing any act, or taking any proceeding, Sunday, Christmas Day, and Good Friday shall not be reckoned in the computation of such limited time"—that the act or proceeding cannot lawfully be done on Sunday, Christmas Day, or Good Friday.

The omission to indorse within the time is a fatal non-compliance with the rules. The writ must be reserved.

The only cases in which judgment can be signed on an affidavit of service not strictly personal on the defendant, are those in which some other mode of service is prescribed by the Judicature or other Acts.

By the Judicature Acts, Order 9, rule 3 : When husband and wife are both defendants to the action, service on the husband shall be deemed good service on the wife; but the Court or a Judge may order that the wife shall be served with or without service on the husband.

Under this Rule, judgment may be signed against the Husband and Wife on an affidavit of personal service on the Husband.

Rule 4. When an infant is a defendant to the action, service on his or her father or guardian, or, if none, then upon the person with whom the infant resides, or under whose care he or she is, shall, unless the Court or Judge otherwise orders, be deemed good service on the infant; provided that the Court or Judge may order that service made or to be made on the infant shall be deemed good service.

Rule 5. When a lunatic or person of unsound mind, not so found by inquisition, is a defendant to the action, service on the committee of the lunatic, or on the person with whom the person of unsound mind resides, or under whose care he or she is, shall, unless the Court or Judge otherwise orders, be deemed good service on such defendant.

The language of these two Rules "shall be deemed good service;" being precisely similar to the preceding one, it might have been assumed that judgment might be signed against the Infant or Lunatic on an affidavit of service in the manner prescribed, but on reference to Order 13, rule 1, it appears that a different procedure is directed.

"Where no appearance has been entered to a writ of summons for a defendant who is an infant or a person of unsound mind, not so found by inquisition, the plaintiff may apply to the Court or a Judge for an order that some proper person be assigned guardian of such defendant, by whom he may appear and defend the action," &c.

From this it seems that judgment for non-appearance cannot be signed under Rules 4 and 5 of Order 9.

Rule 6. "Where partners are sued in the name of their firm, the writ shall be served either upon any one or more of the partners, or at the principal place within the jurisdiction of the business of the partnership, upon any person having at the time of service the control or management of the partnership business there; and, subject to the

Rules hereinafter contained, such service shall be deemed good service upon the firm."

6A. "Where one person carrying on business in the name of a firm, apparently consisting of more than one person, shall be sued in the firm name, the writ may be served at the principal place within the jurisdiction of the business so carried on upon any person having at the time of service the control or management of the business there; and, subject to any of the Rules of the Supreme Court, such service shall be deemed good service on the person so sued."

Under Rule 6, judgment may be signed against the Firm on an affidavit of personal service of the writ on one or more of the partners therein, but it is evidently necessary that the affidavit should give the name or names of the person or persons served, and state that they are members of the firm.

Under Rule 6A, the person trading in the name of a firm having been served, the judgment will be against the Firm and not against the individual.

Under both Rules, judgment may be signed against the Firm on an affidavit of service of the writ on the person having at the time the control or management of the business, but the affidavit should identify, if possible, the person served, and the service must be at the principal place of business within the jurisdiction. This latter condition would prevent this portion of the Rule from applying to writs for service out of the jurisdiction.

The words of the Rule are very wide, and judgment has been signed on an affidavit of service on "the person having the management, &c.," when "the person" was an office boy left in charge, but this was, of course, set aside on application, and although the officer of the Court cannot require in the affidavit more than the words given in the Rule, care must be taken not to stretch them unduly.

The power to sue and be sued in the name of a Firm is a creation of the Judicature Acts, but it should be noted that, to come under the foregoing Rules, the writ must be issued against A. B. & Co., and not against A. B. and C. D. *trading as* A. B. & Co., nor against A. B. *trading as* A. B. & Co.

N.B.—This Rule does not apply to writs issued under the Bills of Exchange Act, *vide post*.

Rule 7. "Whenever, by any statute, provision is made for service of any writ of summons, bill, petition, or other process upon any Corporation, or upon any hundred, or the inhabitants of any place, or any society or fellowship, or any body or number of persons, whether corporate or otherwise, every writ of summons may be served in the manner so provided."

By the Common Law Procedure Act, 1852, s. 16, "Every such writ of summons issued against a corporation aggregate may be served on the mayor or other head officer, or on the town clerk, clerk, treasurer, or secretary of such corporation; and every such writ issued against the inhabitants of a hundred or other like district may be served on the high constable thereof, or any one of the high constables thereof; and every such writ issued against the inhabitants of any county of any city or town, or the inhabitants of any franchise, liberty, city, town or place not being part of a hundred or other like district, on some peace officer thereof."

By the Companies Clauses Act, 8 Vict. c. 16, s. 135, the Lands Clauses Act, 8 Vict. c. 18, s. 134, and the Railways Clauses Act, 8 Vict. c. 20, s. 138, "Any summons or notice, or any writ or other proceeding at law or in equity requiring to be served upon the company, may be served by the same being left at, or transmitted through the post, directed to the principal office of the company, or one of their principal offices when there shall be more than one, or being given personally to the secretary, or, in case there be no secretary, then by being given to any one director of the company."

Therefore, judgment may be signed against any corporation or company coming under any of the foregoing Acts on an affidavit of the service of the writ in any of the modes prescribed.

But under 19 & 20 Vict. c. 47, s. 53 (the Joint Stock Companies Act), which enacts that, "Any summons or notice requiring to be served upon the company may, except in cases where a particular mode of service is directed, be served by leaving the same, or sending it through the post, addressed to the company, at their registered office, or by giving it to any director, secretary, or other principal officer of the company," it was unanimously decided by the Court of Common Pleas in *Towne* v. *The London and Limerick Steamship Company*, 5 C. B. N. S. 730, that the above section did not apply to Writs of Summons, consequently judgment could not be signed on an affidavit of such service.

Mr. Wilson, however, is of opinion that, as it has never been doubted that a bill in Chancery might be served under this section, that will be sufficient to import the section into Rule 7.

Rule 8. "Service of a writ of summons in an action to recover land may, in case of vacant possession, when it cannot otherwise be effected, be made by posting a copy of the writ upon the door of the dwelling-house or other conspicuous part of the property."

Service in compliance with this Rule, which is the same as section 170 of the Common Law Procedure Act, 1852, is not sufficient to entitle the plaintiff to judgment; an order must be obtained as under the old practice.

The remaining Rules of this Order apply to Admiralty actions.

By Order 13, rule 4, "Where there are several

defendants to a writ specially indorsed for a debt or liquidated demand in money, under Order 3, Rule 6, and one or more of them appear to the writ, and another or others of them do not appear, the plaintiff may enter final judgment against such as have not appeared, and may issue execution upon such judgment without prejudice to his right to proceed with his action against such as have appeared." There is no express authority under this or any other Rule to sign judgment for Non-appearance against one or more Defendants when there are others who have not been served or whose time for appearance has not expired, but the practice is to take a judgment for Non-appearance against any Defendant who has been served and has not appeared.

Jurat, and before whom Sworn.

Regulæ Generales, Hilary Term, 1853.

139. In every affidavit made by two or more deponents, the names of the several persons making such affidavit shall be written in the jurat.

140. No affidavit shall be read or made use of in any matter depending in Court in the jurat of which there shall be any interlineation or erasure.

141. When any affidavit is sworn before any Judge or any commissioner by any person, who from his or her signature appears to be illiterate,

the Judge's clerk or commissioner taking such affidavit, shall certify or state in the jurat that the affidavit was read in his presence to the party making the same, and that such party seemed perfectly to understand the same, and also that the said party wrote his or her mark or signature in the presence of the Judge's clerk or commissioner taking the said affidavit.

142. No affidavit of the service of process shall be deemed sufficient if sworn before the plaintiff's own attorney or his clerk.

143. Where an agent in town, or an attorney in the country, is the attorney on the record, an affidavit sworn before the attorney in the country shall not be received; and an affidavit sworn before an attorney's clerk shall not be received in cases where it would not be receivable if sworn before the attorney himself; but this rule shall not extend to affidavits to hold to bail.

144. An affidavit sworn before a Judge of any of the Courts shall be received in the Court to which such Judge belongs, though not entitled of that Court, but not in any other Court, unless entitled of the Court in which it is to be used.

The Date of swearing the affidavit, and the Place and County where it is sworn, must be stated in the Jurat. The place may be stated by reference if it be mentioned in the body of the affidavit. The words, "before me," must be inserted in the jurat if the affidavit is sworn before a commissioner, and the omission of these words cannot be waived.

A line drawn through two words in the jurat, leaving them, however, perfectly legible, is an erasure within Rule 140, and vitiates the affidavit, though the omission or retention of the words would not vary the sense; so is striking out the date mentioned in the jurat with a pen and inserting the right date, according to cases decided; in fact, the Rule applies to any alteration or erasure however slight or unimportant. The Rule is plain and stringent; the Court has always strictly upheld it, and the Officer of the Court has no power to relax it.

"Before me," may be struck out or altered, and the whole jurat may be struck out and a fresh one written.

An alteration in the jurat or other parts of an affidavit after it is sworn nullifies it; it cannot be used. If an interlineation or alteration is made in an affidavit previous to its being sworn, it should be noticed by the person before whom it is sworn, by placing his initials in the margin, for, if the objection is taken, the affidavit cannot be read.

Clerical errors are not considered sufficient ground for rejecting an affidavit when the meaning is clear, but this will depend upon whether the mistake is material or not.

Affidavits have been rejected in which the word "oath," also in which the words " make oath and say," were omitted, and where "said" was substituted for "saith."

Affidavits of service within the jurisdiction may be sworn before the Court, or a Judge, or Commissioner of the Supreme Court, but not before the Plaintiff's Attorney or Agent, or the clerk of either of them. Rules 142 and 143, H. T. 1853. If the writ is served beyond the jurisdiction, the affidavit may be sworn before every British ambassador, envoy, minister, charge d'affaires, or secretary of embassy or of legation exercising his functions in any foreign country, and every British vice-consul, acting-consul, pro-consul, or consular agent (as well as every consul-general or consul), exercising, &c. 18 & 19 Vict. c. 42, ss. 1 and 2. And by section 3, the seal and signature of any British ambassador, consul, &c., as aforesaid, shall be admitted in evidence without proof.

Affidavits may also be made, in a Foreign Country, before a Mayor or other magistrate, or officer there authorised by the law of such country to administer oaths, but in cases not within the Act above mentioned, the signature to the jurat, and also the authority of the person to administer oaths and take affidavits, must be verified by an affidavit made in this country, or by the certificate of a notary public, or a British consul, &c.

An affidavit may be sworn abroad in a foreign language, provided there be an affidavit verifying a translation of it.

Affidavit of Service.

An affidavit sworn before a person having no authority to receive it is a nullity. Age is no objection to an affidavit, unless lapse of time affects the matters contained in it.

By Order 11, rule 5, "Notice in lieu of service shall be given in the manner in which writs of summons are served."

Judgment for non-appearance may be signed on an affidavit of service of the writ or notice beyond the jurisdiction in the same manner as on a service within the jurisdiction.

The Form of judgment for Non-appearance for a liquidated amount will in all cases be No. 1.

CHAPTER II.

JUDGMENT FOR NON-APPEARANCE ON ORDER FOR SUBSTITUTED SERVICE, WHEN THE WRIT IS SPECIALLY ENDORSED.

Order 9, rule 2. " When service is required the writ shall, wherever it is practicable, be served in the manner in which personal service is now made, but if it be made to appear to the Court or to a Judge that the plaintiff is from any cause unable to effect prompt personal service, the Court or Judge may make such order for substituted or other service, or for the substitution of notice for service, as may seem just."

In every case in which the writ is not served on the Defendant personally, or in one of the modes prescribed by the Rules, an order for substituted or other service must be obtained in the manner directed by Order 10.

"Every application to the Court or a Judge under Order 9, Rule 2, for an order for substituted or other service, or for the substitution of notice for service, shall be supported by an affidavit setting forth the grounds upon which the application is made."

This order must be served (and generally together with a copy of the writ) in the manner directed by the order itself, and the Defendant will have the same time to appear from the service of the order as he would have had if the writ had been personally served on that day.

The original order must be filed on signing judgment, with an affidavit that the directions of the order have been complied with; that is, that a copy of the order and a copy of the writ (if so directed) have been served at the place, and in the manner ordered.

The writ and a certificate of non-appearance dated the day of signing judgment must be produced.

The judgment will be in the same form as the ordinary judgment for non-appearance.

CHAPTER III.

JUDGMENT FOR NON-APPEARANCE WHERE THE PLAINTIFF'S CLAIM IS FOR A LIQUIDATED DEMAND, BUT THE WRIT IS NOT SPECIALLY INDORSED.

Order 13, rule 5. "Where the defendant fails to appear to the writ of summons, and the writ is not specially indorsed, but the plaintiff's claim is for a debt or liquidated demand only, no statement of claim need be delivered, but the plaintiff may file an affidavit of service, or notice in lieu of service, as the case may be, and a statement of the particulars of his claim in respect of the causes of action stated in the indorsement upon the writ, and may, after the expiration of eight days, enter final judgment for the amount shown thereby, and costs to be taxed, provided that the amount shall not be more than the sum indorsed upon the writ besides costs."

Where the Plaintiff's claim is for a liquidated amount, but the writ is not specially indorsed in compliance with Order 3, rule 6, so as to

Judgment for Non-Appearance.

entitle him to immediate judgment for non-appearance, the proceedings will be under this Rule.

The Plaintiff, having complied with the Rule, may take a judgment for non-appearance after the expiration of eight days from the filing of the particulars, exclusive of the day of filing. No notice of the filing need be given to the Defendant, and, as the advantages of specially indorsing the writ, in compliance with Order 3, rule 6, become more generally recognized, it is probable that cases under this Rule will be few and far between. When the writ has not been personally served, and an order for substituted service has been procured, the particulars may be filed with the affidavit of the service of the order.

The sufficiency of the indorsement on the writ to entitle the Plaintiff to immediate judgment is not at all affected by the granting of an order for substituted service.

A memorandum of the date of filing the particulars, and affidavit or order, should be made on the judgment, and a certificate of non-appearance, dated the day of signing judgment, must be produced.

The Form will be the same as the ordinary judgment for non-appearance.

CHAPTER IV.

JUDGMENT FOR NON-APPEARANCE WHEN THE PLAINTIFF'S CLAIM IS UNLIQUIDATED.

Order 13, rule 6. " Where the defendant fails to appear to the writ of summons, and the plaintiff's claim is not for a debt or liquidated demand only, but for detention of goods and pecuniary damages, or either of them, no statement of claim need be delivered, but interlocutory judgment may be entered, and a writ of inquiry shall issue to assess the value of the goods and the damages, or the damages only, as the case may be, in respect of the causes of action disclosed by the indorsement on the writ of summons. But the Court, or a Judge, may order that, instead of a writ of inquiry, the value and amount of damages, or either of them, shall be ascertained in any way in which any question arising in an action may be tried."

This Rule, although at first sight, and from the prominence given to claims for "detention of goods, and pecuniary damages," it might have been thought to apply to actions of Detinue only, governs the practice in all cases of claims for unliquidated damages which are not provided for by any other Rule.

All judgments under this Rule, according to the words of it, must be interlocutory; but it would seem that, where the action is brought for the specific recovery of chattels, the Plaintiff may take a judgment on non-appearance for the recovery of the chattels, and upon this a writ of delivery may issue. *Ivory* v. *Cruikshank*, at Chambers, W. N., 1875, p. 249. Where the claim is for specific recovery, and, in the alternative, for damages, probably two judgments would have to be signed, one, final, for the recovery of the goods, and the other, interlocutory, to assess their value.

In all ordinary actions for damages, interlocutory judgment would be signed under this Rule, and the damages afterwards assessed by writ of inquiry, or reference to the Master, or as the Court or a Judge may direct.

The Form will be No. 5.

CHAPTER V.

JUDGMENT FOR NON-APPEARANCE FOR THE RECOVERY OF LAND ALONE, OR FOR THE RECOVERY OF LAND AND MESNE PROFITS, ARREARS OF RENT, OR DAMAGES FOR BREACH OF CONTRACT.

Order 13, rule 7. "In case no appearance shall be entered in an action for the recovery of land, within the time limited for appearance, or if an appearance be entered but the defence be limited to part only, the plaintiff shall be at liberty to enter a judgment that the person whose title is asserted in the writ shall recover possession of the land, or of the part thereof to which the defence does not apply."

Rule 8. "Where the plaintiff has indorsed a claim for mesne profits, arrears of rent, or damages for breach of contract, upon a writ for the recovery of land, he may enter judgment as in the last preceding Rule mentioned for the land; and may proceed as in the other preceding Rules of this order as to such other claim so indorsed."

Judgment for Non-appearance for the possession of land or premises alone is signed in the same manner as for the recovery of a debt, except as to the Form of the Judgment, which will be No. 2, the same as given in the Appendix to the Act.

The writ must be served in the same way as any other writ—that is, upon the Defendant, or all the defendants named in the writ, personally. The whole of the defendants should be served before Judgment is taken. If there are several defendants, and one or more of them appear, and others do not, or if a person not named in the writ appears and defends, by leave of the Court or a Judge, under Order 12, rule 18, judgment for non-appearance should be taken against all those defendants who do not appear. This judgment cannot be enforced so long as there is a defence outstanding to the action, but when judgment has been obtained against the defendant or defendants who appear, a writ of possession may issue on the judgment for non-appearance against the defendants named therein.

Service under Order 9, rule 8 (*ante*, p. 20), does not entitle the Plaintiff to judgment. An order must be obtained.

According to the Form, the judgment for possession does not carry costs.

If the indorsement on the writ comprises some or all of the various claims which, by Rule 8, are allowed to be added to a claim for the recovery of

D

land, there will be two judgments—one, final, for the recovery of the land, and also (if the particulars of this portion of the claim are duly indorsed according to Order 3, rule 6) for the arrears of rent; the other, interlocutory, for the mesne profits and damages for breach of contract, which are to be recovered as directed by "preceding rules of this Order," *vide* Rule 6.

The two judgments must be taken at the same time, as they are grounded on the same documents, the affidavit or order for substituted service, and these can only be used once.

When the amount recovered for arrears of rent, in addition to possession, exceeds £20, judgment may be signed for the usual amount of costs on non-appearance.

The final judgment for possession of the land and arrears of rent will be in Form No. 3; the interlocutory for mesne profits or damages in Form No. 4.

CHAPTER VI.

JUDGMENT FOR NON-APPEARANCE UNDER THE BILLS OF EXCHANGE ACT.

By Order 2, rule 6, of the Judicature Acts, " With respect to actions upon a bill of exchange or promissory note, commenced within six months after the same shall have become due and payable, the procedure under the Bills of Exchange Act, 18 & 19 Vict. c. 67, shall continue to be used."

The judgment for Non-appearance under the Bills of Exchange Act is similar to that under the Judicature Act, but there are important differences in the procedure.

By Sec. 6, " The holder of any bill of exchange or promissory note may, if he think fit, issue one writ of summons according to this Act against all or any number of the parties to such bill or note, and such writ of summons shall be the commencement of an action or actions against the parties therein named respectively; and all subsequent proceedings against such respective parties shall be in like manner—so far as may be, as if separate writs of summons had been issued."

The power to include all the parties to a bill of exchange or promissory note in one writ was entirely new at the time of passing the Bills of Exchange Act. It could not be done under the Common Law Procedure Act, and, although by the Judicature Act, Order 16, rule 5, "the Plaintiff may, at his option, join as parties to the same action all or any of the persons severally, or jointly and severally liable on any one contract, including parties to bills of exchange and promissory notes," there is no provision for one writ being the commencement of several actions.

Under the above Rule, a joint judgment may be taken against the several parties to a bill or note, but, under the Bills of Exchange Act, this cannot be done, for, although all parties may be included in one writ, "subsequent proceedings shall be as if separate writs had been issued." A joint judgment may be taken against any two or more drawers, acceptors, or indorsers, but drawer and acceptor, or two several indorsers, cannot be included in one judgment. When the writ contains the names of all the parties and separate judgments are taken, the judgment should be drawn as if the writ had been issued against the party proceeded against only, the name of the other parties should not appear on it; and the Affidavit of service should be similarly intitled.

A separate certificate of non-appearance must be produced for each judgment. The Bills of Exchange Act requires a copy of the writ to be filed with the Affidavit or order to proceed, on signing judgment, but this is not now insisted on, as a copy must be filed on issuing the writ, under the Judicature Act.

The proceedings where the writ has not been personally served are also different; the old form of order is retained, and this is that " three days after service of a copy of this order at   , the Plaintiff shall be at liberty to proceed in this action as if personal service of the writ of summons had been effected upon the defendant."

This is entirely different to the order for substituted service, and judgment may be signed after the expiration of three days, exclusive of the date of the order.

The indorsement of the service must be made on the back of the order by the person serving it, and no affidavit is necessary.

There is another important difference between the proceedings by default of appearance under the Judicature Act and the Bills of Exchange Act. By the decision of the Exchequer Division in *Pollock & anr.* v. *Campell Bros.*, L. R. E. D., 1876, Part 3, p. 50, it has been held that Order 9, rule 6, of the former does not apply to proceedings under the latter. In the Bills of Exchange Act there is no provision for suing partners in the name of their firm, and every defendant must be personally described and personally served. Under sec. 4 of the Common Law Procedure Act, 1852, which is incorporated with the Bills of Exchange Act, " Every writ of summons shall contain the names of all the defendants," and even if a writ could be issued against *A. B. & Co.*, as the rule of the Judicature Act does not apply, it could not be served on " the above named defendants ———."

CHAPTER VII.

JUDGMENT FOR NON-APPEARANCE WHERE THE APPEARANCE IS STRUCK OUT OR SET ASIDE BY ORDER.

When the order is simply to strike out or set aside the appearance, the judgment will be for Non-appearance as if no appearance had been entered; and an affidavit or order for substituted service must be filed, and a certificate of non-appearance produced.

The Form will be No. 6.

When the order directs that the appearance be struck out, and the Plaintiff be at liberty to sign Judgment, Judgment may be signed on the order without any further authority. The order should state for what amount judgment is to be signed, but if no amount is mentioned, it may be assumed to be that claimed on the writ.

The Form in this case will be No. 19.

CHAPTER VIII.

JUDGMENT UNDER ORDER 14, RULE 1.

Order 14, rule 1. " Where the defendant appears to a writ of summons specially indorsed under Order 3, Rule 6, the plaintiff may, on affidavit made by himself, or by any other person who can swear positively to the debt or cause of action— verifying the cause of action, and stating that in his belief there is no defence to the action—call on the defendant to show cause before the Court or a Judge why the Plaintiff should not be at liberty to sign final judgment for the amount so indorsed, together with interest, if any, and costs. A copy of the affidavit shall accompany the summons or notice of motion. The Court or a Judge may thereupon, unless the defendant, by affidavit or otherwise, satisfy the Court or a Judge that he has a good defence to the action on the merits, or disclose such facts as may be deemed sufficient to entitle him to defend, make an order empowering the plaintiff to sign judgment accordingly."

It must be noted that in order to entitle the Plaintiff to apply to sign judgment under this Rule the writ must be specially indorsed under Order 3, rule 6, as to the importance of which indorsement see Judgment for Non-appearance, p. 8, *ante*.

If the Defendant appears, and the Plaintiff, under this and the following Rules of the same Order, applies for and obtains an order to be at liberty to sign judgment notwithstanding such appearance, the order made by the Master is usually—

1. That the Plaintiff be at liberty to sign judgment for the amount indorsed on the Writ with interest, if any, and costs, or for an amount specified, absolutely.

2. That unless certain conditions (generally the payment of money into Court within a given time) are complied with, the Plaintiff shall be at liberty to sign judgment, &c.

3. That the Plaintiff shall have immediate judgment for part of his claim, and the Defendant shall have leave, with or without conditions, to defend as to the residue.

4. That the Plaintiff shall have immediate judgment for the amount of his claim against one or more of the Defendants, without prejudice to his right to proceed against the others.

When the amount for which judgment is to be signed is given, the production of the order is the only authority necessary to sign judgment under Order 14, rule 1, but when the judgment is to be for "the amount indorsed on the writ, with interest, if any," the writ must be produced to show the amount indorsed, and whether interest was claimed.

In the 1st, 3rd, and 4th cases, Form No. 7 may be used, but in the 2nd case the conditions of the order must be set out on the judgment, and Form No. 8 will apply.

CHAPTER IX.

JUDGMENT FOR WANT OF STATEMENT OF DEFENCE.

The Plaintiff may be entitled to sign judgment for non-delivery of Statement of Defence under the following rules :—

Order 19, rule 2. "Unless the defendant in an action at the time of his appearance shall state that he does not require the delivery of a statement of complaint, the plaintiff shall within such time and in such manner as hereinafter prescribed, deliver to the defendant after his appearance a statement of his complaint, and of the relief or remedy to which he claims to be entitled. The defendant shall within such time and in such manner as hereinafter prescribed deliver to the plaintiff a statement of his defence, set off, or counterclaim (if any), and the plaintiff shall in like manner deliver a statement of his reply (if any) to such defence, set off, or counterclaim. Such statements shall be as brief as the nature of the case will admit, and the Court in adjusting the costs of the action shall inquire at the instance of any party into any unnecessary prolixity, and order the costs occasioned by such prolixity to be borne by the party chargeable with the same."

Order 21, rule 4. "Where the writ is specially indorsed, and the defendant has not dispensed with a statement of claim, it shall be sufficient for the plaintiff to deliver as his statement of claim a notice to the effect that his claim is that which appears by the indorsement upon the writ, unless the Court or a Judge shall order him to deliver a further statement. Such notice may be either written or printed, or partly written and partly printed, and may be in the form No. 3 in Appendix (B) hereto (*a*), and shall be marked on the face in the same manner as is required in the case of an ordinary statement of claim. And when the plaintiff is ordered to deliver

(*a*).   Appendix B. Form 3.

Notice in lieu of Statement of Claim.

187   . (*here put letter and number*).

In the High Court of Justice,
———— Division.

Between *A. B.* - - Plaintiff.
      and
    C. D. - - Defendant.

The particulars of the plaintiff's complaint herein, and of the relief and remedy to which he claims to be entitled, appear by the indorsement upon the writ of summons.

such further statement it shall be delivered within such time as by such order shall be directed, and if no time be so limited, then within the time prescribed by rule 1 of this Order.

Order 22, rule 1. Where a statement of claim is delivered to a defendant, he shall deliver his defence within eight days from the delivery of the statement of claim, or from the time limited for appearance, whichever shall be last, unless such time is extended by the Court or a Judge.

Rule 2. A defendant who has appeared in an action, and stated that he does not require the delivery of a statement of claim, and to whom a statement of claim is not delivered, may deliver a defence at any time within eight days after his appearance, unless such time is extended by the Court or a Judge.

Rule 3. Where leave has been given to a defendant to defend under Order 14, rule 1, he shall deliver his defence, if any, within such time as shall be limited by the order giving him leave to defend, or if no time is thereby limited, then within eight days after the order.

Order 29, rule 2. If the plaintiff's claim be only for a debt or liquidated demand, and the defendant does not, within the time allowed for that purpose, deliver a defence or demurrer, the plaintiff may, at the expiration of such time, enter final judgment for the amount claimed, with costs.

Rule 3. When in any such action as in the last preceding Rule mentioned there are several defendants, if one of them make default as mentioned in the last preceding Rule, the plaintiff may enter final judgment against the defendant so making default, and issue execution upon such judgment without prejudice to his right to proceed with his action against the other defendants.

Rule 4. If the plaintiff's claim be for detention of goods and pecuniary damages, or either of them, and the defendant makes default as mentioned in Rule 2, the plaintiff may enter an interlocutory judgment against the defendant, and a writ of inquiry shall issue to assess the value of the goods, and the damages, or the damages only, as the case may be. But the Court or a Judge may order that, instead of a writ of inquiry, the value and amount of damages, or either of them, shall be ascertained in any way in which any question arising in an action may be tried.

Rule 5. When in any such action as in Rule 4 mentioned there are several defendants, if one of them make default as mentioned in Rule 2 the plaintiff may enter an interlocutory judgment against the defendant so making default, and proceed with his action against the others. And in such case, damages against the defendant making default shall be assessed at the same time with the trial of the action or issues therein against the other defendants, unless the Court or a Judge shall otherwise direct.

Rule 6. If the plaintiff's claim be for a debt or liquidated demand, and also for detention of goods and pecuniary damages, or pecuniary damages only, and the defendant makes default as mentioned in Rule 2, the plaintiff may enter final judgment for the debt or liquidated demand, and also enter interlocutory judgment for the value of the goods and damages, or the damages only, as the case may be, and proceed as mentioned in Rule 4.

Rule 7. In an action for the recovery of land, if the defendant makes default as mentioned in Rule 2, the plaintiff may enter a judgment that the person whose title is asserted in the writ of summons shall recover possession of the land, with his costs.

Rule 8. Where the plaintiff has endorsed a claim for mesne profits, arrears of rent, or damages for breach of contract upon a writ for the recovery of land, if the defendant makes default as mentioned in Rule 2, or, if there be more than one defendant, some or one of the defendants make such default, the plaintiff may enter judgment against the defaulting defendant or defendants, and proceed as mentioned in Rules 4 and 5.

By the subsequent Rules of this Order, if the Defendant makes default in pleading in any case other than those mentioned in the preceding

Rules, the action must be set down on motion for judgment (*vide post*, p. 77), therefore judgment cannot be taken by default.

In the ordinary case, where the Plaintiff's claim is liquidated, and he has delivered a statement of claim, or notice in lieu thereof, under Order 21, rule 4, and is entitled to judgment for non-delivery of defence under Order 29, rules 2 and 3, the Form will be No. 9, as given in the appendix to the Act.

Under Rules 4 and 5 the judgment will be in Form No. 10.

Under Rule 6 there will be two judgments, one final, for the liquidated portion of the claim in Form No. 9, and the other interlocutory, for the unliquidated damages, as in Form No. 10.

Under Rule 7 the Form will be No. 9.

Under Rule 8, if the claim includes mesne profits, arrears of rent, and damages for breach of contract, in addition to the recovery of land, the arrears of rent may be added to the judgment for possession, as this part of the claim is liquidated and might be specially indorsed, but a separate interlocutory judgment must be taken for the mesne profits and damages for breach of contract, which are unliquidated and must be assessed.

In all these cases a statement of claim (or a notice in lieu thereof under Order 21, rule 4) must have been delivered, and a copy of it must be filed on signing judgment.

Under Order 22, rule 2, where the defendant

does not require a statement of claim he may deliver a statement of defence within eight days after appearance; and "may" has been held to mean, in this place, "shall," or there would be no authority for a Judgment.

The decision of J. Lindley, at Chambers, in *Hooper* v. *Giles*, W. N. 1876, p. 10, that the Defendant was not bound to deliver a defence, and the cause must go to trial without pleadings, has been subsequently reversed by J. Blackburn in *Harrison* v. *The Surrey Masonic Hall Co.*, also at Chambers, 21 June, 1876, and the practice now is that, when the Defendant appears and dispenses with a statement of claim, and does not deliver a statement of defence within eight days from his appearance, the Plaintiff may take a judgment by default. In this case the Form is No. 11.

Under Order 22, rule 3, it has been decided by J. Lindley, at Chambers, in *Atkins* v. *Taylor*, W. N. 1876, p. 11, that this Rule overrides Order 19, rule 2, and the Defendant must deliver a statement of defence within eight days after the date of the order giving him leave to defend, although no statement of claim has been delivered, otherwise the Plaintiff may take a judgment by default.

When judgment is signed under this Rule it should so appear on the face of it, as in Form No. 12.

Where the Defendant has delivered a statement of defence in due course, and this statement has been struck out by Judge's order, if the order simply directs that the pleading be struck out, judgment may be signed by default as if it had never been delivered, for the amount claimed if liquidated, or for damages to be assessed, as in Form No. 13.

When the order goes on to say that the Plaintiff shall be at liberty to sign judgment for an amount stated, the judgment is on the order and the Form will be No. 19.

If the order is conditional, *e.g.*, that unless the defendant files answers to interrogatories, or complies with some other directions of the Judge, his defence shall be struck out, the conditions and the non-compliance with them should be stated in the judgment, as in Form No. 14.

CHAPTER X.

JUDGMENT FOR NOT ENTERING DEMURRER FOR ARGUMENT.

Order 28, rule 6. When a demurrer either to the whole or part of a pleading is delivered, either party may enter the demurrer for argument immediately, and the party so entering such demurrer shall on the same day give notice thereof to the other party. If the demurrer shall not be entered and notice thereof given within ten days after delivery, and if the party whose pleading is demurred to does not within such time serve an order for leave to amend, the demurrer shall be held sufficient for the same purposes and with the same result as to costs as if it had been allowed on argument.

Under this Rule, a party whose pleading is demurred to, and who does not within ten days from the delivery of the demurrer serve an order for leave to amend, or enter the demurrer for argument, and give notice to the opposite party, is placed in the same position as if the demurrer had been heard and allowed, that is, judgment may be signed against him. Either party may enter the demurrer for argument, but it is not likely the one delivering it would do so, as he will be as well off if it is not entered as if it is allowed.

Judgment may be either for the Plaintiff or the Defendant, and, like all judgments for default of a pleading, must be signed on the responsibility of the Solicitor, no evidence of default having been made being required by the Officer of the Court.

When the party demurring is the Plaintiff, and the demurrer is to the whole defence, if the Defendant does not enter it or serve an order to amend, the Plaintiff may sign judgment for all he would have been entitled to recover if no defence had been delivered.

In this case the Form will be No. 16.

When the Defendant demurs, and the Plaintiff does not enter it, the Defendant may sign judgment for his costs as he would on a Rule for Judgment on Demurrer.

The Form will be No. 17.

CHAPTER XI.

JUDGMENT ON CONFESSION OF DEFENCE.

Order 20, rule 3. Whenever any defendant, in his statement of defence, or in any further statement of defence as in the last Rule mentioned, alleges any ground of defence which has arisen after the commencement of the action, the plaintiff may deliver a confession of such defence, which confession may be in the Form No. 2 in Appendix (B) hereto (*a*), with such variations as circumstances may require, and he may thereupon sign judgment for his costs up to the time of the

---

(*a*). Appendix B. Form 2.

Confession by Plaintiff of Defence.

18 . (*here put the letter and number*).
In the High Court.
Queen's Bench Division.
Between *A. B.* - - Plaintiff.
and
C. D. - - Defendant.

The Plaintiff confesses the defence stated in the paragraph of the defendant's statement of defence (or of the defendant's further statement of defence).

pleading of such defence, unless the Court or a Judge shall, either before or after the delivery of such confession, otherwise order.

This Rule is similar to the old practice. The procedure necessary to obtain a judgment under it is sufficiently defined by the Rule itself, and the Form will be No. 15.

CHAPTER XII.

JUDGMENT ON TAKING MONEY OUT OF COURT.

Order 30, rule 1. Where any action is brought to recover a debt or damages, any defendant may, at any time after service of the writ, and before or at the time of delivering his defence, or by leave of the Court or a Judge at any later time, pay into Court a sum of money by way of satisfaction or amends. Payment into Court shall be pleaded in the defence, and the claim or cause of action in respect of which such payment shall be made shall be specified therein.

Rule 4. The Plaintiff, if payment into Court is made before delivering a defence, may, within four days after receipt of notice of such payment, or if such payment is first stated in a defence delivered then may before reply, accept the same in satisfaction of the causes of action, in respect of which it is paid in; in which case he shall give notice to the defendant in the Form No. 6 in Appendix

(B) hereto (*a*), and shall be at liberty, in case the sum paid in is accepted in satisfaction of the entire cause of action, to tax his costs, and, in case of non-payment within forty-eight hours, to sign judgment for his costs so taxed.

Under Rule 1 (*suprà*), money may now be paid into Court by way of satisfaction or amends in any action brought to recover a debt or damages, whereas, under the old practice, there were several exceptions. The money having been paid in, the Plaintiff may, as a matter of course, take it out of Court, and accept it either in full satisfaction of his claim, or of any portion of his claim, or in part satisfaction, and proceed with his action for the remainder; but it is only in case he accepts it in satisfaction of the entire cause of action, that he will be entitled, under Rule 4, to tax his costs, and sign judgment for them, if they are not paid within forty-eight hours after taxation.

(*a*). Appendix B. Form 6.

Acceptance of Sum paid into Court.

1875. B. No.

In the High Court of Justice,
    Q. B. Division.

A. B. *v.* C. D.

Take notice that the plaintiff accepts the sum of £——— paid by you into Court in satisfaction of the claim in respect of which it is paid in.

In this case the judgment will be in Form No. 18.

The judgment should be signed, leaving the amount of costs blank, and an allocatur afterwards taken for the whole amount of costs, including those of judgment.

CHAPTER XIII.

JUDGMENT ON JUDGE'S ORDER.

A Judge's order to sign Judgment may be obtained at any stage of the proceedings. It is usually made by consent of the parties, and embodies an agreement between them to stay proceedings upon payment of a certain sum, with costs to be taxed, on a certain date, or by instalments, with liberty to the Plaintiff to sign Judgment upon default being made in any payment. This is the old "order to stay," and Judgment may be signed under it in Form No. 19; if there are any pleadings in the action, a copy of them must be filed. If the payment of the debt with costs to be taxed, is directed, the costs up to and including the order should be taxed, as default in payment cannot be made until the amount to be paid has been ascertained. On signing Judgment the original order with the allocatur on it must be produced, but not filed. The costs taxed on the order should not be inserted in the judgment, but a fresh allocatur for the whole costs, including those of the judgment, should be taken on the solicitor's copy of the Judgment, after it is signed; and this should then be brought to the officer for the amount to be filled in the original.

This is the commonest form of order, and the terms may vary in many ways, but, whatever they are, they must be set out on the judgment. But it may be necessary to obtain an order to sign judgment in many other circumstances, and for various reasons; for instance, on a question arising out of the pleadings, on an award, when the order of reference does not contain an authority to sign judgment on the award, on the Master's certificate under 17 & 18 Vict. c. 125, s. 3, but in the latter case the judgment is not on the order but on the certificate, *vide post*.

No judgment can be signed on an order unless the order distinctly directs a judgment, and the amount for which it may be signed should also be given, either expressly or by reference. When the order is merely a permission to sign judgment on some other document or authority, the judgment is signed on the previous authority. The date of the order, its contents, and the name of the Judge or Master making it must always appear on the Judgment.

CHAPTER XIV.

JUDGMENT ON WARRANT OF ATTORNEY AND COGNOVIT.

The Judicature Acts and Rules are silent as to the procedure on Warrant of Attorney and Cognovit, which therefore remains unaltered, by virtue of sec. 21 of the Act of 1875, but is now very rarely resorted to.

The original Warrant must be filed on signing Judgment, and it is the duty of the officer to see that it is duly executed and stamped; an appearance must be entered before signing judgment, which is for the penalty in the Warrant, with an allowance of £3 10s. for costs without taxation.

Judgment may be signed as a matter of course at any time within a year from the date of the Warrant, but afterwards only by order of a Judge.

The Form will be No. 20.

Cognovits are now entirely disused in actions for debt, but are occasionally given in actions for the recovery of land, when a person not named in the writ has obtained leave to appear and defend, and afterwards wishes to suffer a Judgment. This may be done by a notice of confession, under secs. 203, 204, 205 of the Common Law Procedure Act, 1852, and is the simplest mode of getting a Judgment.

The Form will be No. 21.

CHAPTER XV.

JUDGMENT ON MASTER'S CERTIFICATE.

There are two kinds of reference to the Master on which Judgment may be signed, one under the Common Law Procedure Act, 1854, secs. 3, 9 and 10, and one under the Common Law Procedure Act, 1852, sec. 94; and the Judicature Act, Order 13, rule 6, and Order 29, rule 4.

By 17 & 18 Vict. c. 125 (C. L. P. A., 1854), s. 3, if it be made appear, at any time after the issuing of the writ, to the satisfaction of the Court or a Judge, upon the application of either party, that the matter in dispute consists wholly or in part of matters of mere account which cannot conveniently be tried in the ordinary way, it shall be lawful for such Court or Judge upon such application, if they or he think fit, to decide such matter in a summary manner, or to order that such matter, either wholly or in part, be referred to an arbitrator appointed by the parties, or to an officer of the Court, upon such terms as to costs and otherwise as such Court or Judge shall think reasonable; and the decision or order of such Court or Judge, or the award or certificate of such referee, shall be enforceable by the same process as the finding of a jury upon the matter referred.

The reference under this section is compulsory, and may be made on the application of either party; it is usually to one of the Masters of the Court, although it may be to any other arbitrator with the same powers. The award or certificate is enforceable by the same process as the finding of a jury, or rather as the finding of a jury was at the passing of the Act, that is, by judgment and execution, but judgment cannot be signed immediately, the time is regulated by the following sections:—

S. 9. All applications to set aside any award made on a compulsory reference under this Act shall and may be made within the first seven days of the term next following the publication of the award to the parties, whether made in vacation or term; and if no such application is made, or if no rule is granted thereon, or if any rule granted thereon is afterwards discharged, such award shall be final between the parties.

S. 10. Any award made on a compulsory reference under this Act may, by authority of a Judge, on such terms as to him may seem reasonable, be enforced at any time after seven days from the time of publication, notwithstanding that the time for moving to set it aside has not elapsed.

Practically, therefore, the party in whose favour

the certificate is, always avails himself of this last section, and obtains, as a matter of course, an order to be at liberty to sign judgment on the certificate, not less than seven days after the date of it, although, if he choose to wait, he may still avail himself of section 9, the old Terms being still retained as measures of time within which any act is to be done, by sec. 26 of the Judicature Act.

The Master's certificate and the subsequent order must be produced on signing judgment, and the Form will be No. 22.

The other kind of reference to the Master is, instead of a Writ of Inquiry, under the Common Law Procedure Act, 1852, sec. 94—

"In actions in which it shall appear to the Court or a Judge that the amount of damages sought to be recovered by the plaintiff is substantially a matter of calculation, it shall not be necessary to issue a writ of inquiry, but the Court or a Judge may direct that the amount for which final judgment is to be signed shall be ascertained by one of the Masters of the said Court; and the attendance of witnesses and the production of documents before such Master may be compelled by subpœna, in the same manner as before a Jury upon a writ of inquiry; and it shall be lawful for such Master to adjourn the inquiry from time to time as occasion may require; and the Master shall indorse upon the rule or order for referring the amount of damages to him, the amount found by him, and shall deliver the rule or order with such indorsement to the plaintiff; and such and the like proceedings may thereupon be had as to taxation of costs, signing judgment, and otherwise, as upon the finding of a jury upon a writ of inquiry."

By Order 13, rule 6, and Order 29, rule 4, of the Judicature Act (*ante*, pp. 30, 46) in actions for damages after interlocutory judgment by default of appearance or defence, the Court or a Judge may order that, instead of a writ of inquiry, the amount of damages shall be ascertained in any way in which any question arising in an action may be tried.

By sec. 94, C. L. P. A., 1852, the Master is to indorse on the order the amount found by him, and deliver it to the plaintiff, and the like proceedings may be had thereupon, as to signing judgment, &c., as on the finding of a jury on a writ of inquiry; and by Rule 55 of Hilary Term, 1853, " No rule for judgment shall be necessary; and after the return of a writ of inquiry judgment may be signed at the expiration of four days from such return." It seems, therefore, that judgment should not be signed until after the expiration of four days from the date of the Master's certificate. By the section, the Master is to indorse his certificate on the order, and by another Rule, 171, of Hilary Term, 1853, "On a reference to the Master to ascertain the amount for which final judgment may be signed, the Master's certificate

F

shall be filed in the office when judgment is signed."

In this case, therefore, and in this case only, the order and certificate must be filed on signing judgment.

The Form will be No. 23.

CHAPTER XVI.

JUDGMENT ON WRIT OF INQUIRY.

The Rules of the Judicature Act, although by Order 13, rule 6, and Order 29, rule 4, they provide for the issuing of a Writ of Inquiry, where the Plaintiff's claim is for unliquidated damages, are entirely silent as to how a judgment is to be obtained upon it. The old practice, therefore, remains unchanged, and this is governed by Rule 55 of Hilary Term, 1853, which has just been quoted with reference to judgment on the Master's certificate, but it may, perhaps, be as well to set it out again here in its proper place.

"No rule for judgment shall be necessary, and after the return of a writ of inquiry judgment may be signed at the expiration of four days from such return."

The return is the return day in the writ, and not the date of the Inquisition.

The production of the Writ and Inquisition is sufficient authority for the judgment, and the Form will be No. 24.

CHAPTER XVII.

JUDGMENT ON COUNTY COURT CERTIFICATE.

By the 19 & 20 Vict. c. 108, s. 26, "Where, in any action of contract brought in a superior Court, the claim indorsed on the writ does not exceed fifty pounds, or where such claim, although it originally exceeded fifty pounds, is reduced by payment into Court payment, an admitted set-off, or otherwise to a sum not exceeding fifty pounds, a Judge of a superior Court on the application of either party, after issue joined, may, in his discretion, and on such terms as he shall think fit, order that the cause be tried in any County Court which he shall name; and thereupon the plaintiff shall lodge with the registrar of such Court such order and the issue, and the Judge of such Court shall appoint a day for the hearing of the cause, notice whereof shall be sent, by post or otherwise, by the registrar to both parties, or their attorneys; and, after such hearing, the registrar shall certify the result to the Master's office of such superior Court, and judgment in accordance with such certificate may be signed in such superior Court."

The Registrar of the County Court in which the cause was ordered to be tried having sent to the Master's Office of the Division of the High Court of Justice in which the action was commenced, his certificate of the result of the trial, the certificate is filed in the Judgment Department, and judgment may be signed in accordance therewith immediately. *Scott* v. *Freeman*, L. R. 2 Q. B. D. 177.

The certificate must state the amount (if any) for which judgment is given, and a copy of the pleadings must be filed on signing judgment. It is important to notice that the section expressly limits to £50 the amount which may be dealt with by the County Court Judge, and a certificate giving a judgment for a larger amount cannot be acted on.

When the amount indorsed on the writ originally exceeded £50, and has been reduced in any of the ways mentioned in the section, the certificate should show a judgment for the amount in dispute only.

The result of the trial, and consequently the judgment, may be in favour either of the plaintiff or the defendant, and Form No. 25 may be adapted to either case.

CHAPTER XVIII.

JUDGMENT ON AWARD.

Besides the references to a Master, and to a County Court Judge, already mentioned, there are other cases in which judgment may be signed on the award of an arbitrator, provided a power to do so is contained in the order of reference. A cause may be referred at any stage of the proceedings, with the consent of the parties, by an order made at Chambers, or by the Judge at the Trial, or a verdict may be taken subject to a reference.

There is an entirely new kind of reference created by the Judicature Acts, that to an Official Referee; but as no judgment can be signed on his report without the authority of the Court, it need not be noticed here, but will be found under judgment by Rule of Court, *post*.

In the case of a reference at Chambers, by consent, the order usually contains a clause that, "unless restrained by any Rule or Order of this Court, or of a Judge of any of the Superior Courts, the Party or Parties in whose favour the said award shall be made shall be at liberty —— days after service of a copy of the said Award on the other Party's Attorney or Agent to sign final judgment for any sum or sums of money found due to him or them by the said Award, and for all costs that he may be entitled to under this order, and under the said Award, together with the costs of the said Judgment;" and under this claim, judgment is signed at any time after the expiration of the time mentioned for the service of the copy of the award. Although the practice in references of this class is still governed by the Common Law Procedure Act, and is not directly affected by the Judicature Act, important modifications have arisen. Now, as formerly, the reference may be of the action alone, or of the action and all matters in difference. In the latter case, under the old practice, judgment could only be signed for the amount found due in the action, and if the award went beyond the subject matter of the action, that portion of it could only be enforced by other process, or by a fresh action. Now it is contended that the words of the order "any sum or sums of money found due to him" entitle the successful party to sign judgment for the whole of the award. The arbitrator may also find an amount to be due from the Plaintiff to the Defendant, and judgment may be signed for it. Whilst, under the old practice, the Defendant in an action could not recover damages from the

Plaintiff, he may now recover, by counterclaim, every thing he might have recovered in an original action against the Plaintiff.

When the reference is of this class, judgment may be signed in Form No. 27, which may be adapted to meet the case of a finding either for the Plaintiff or the Defendant.

When the cause is referred after coming on for Trial at *Nisi Prius*, without a verdict being taken, the order is similar to the preceding, and the old practice is followed with the same differences. But when a verdict is taken subject to a reference, the procedure is entirely changed. In this case, under the old practice, the Arbitrator would have been considered to be in the place of the Jury, and the *postea* would have been made up in accordance with his award as if it had been their Verdict, and upon that judgment would have been signed. According to the present practice although the jury may have been sworn, and a nominal verdict taken, the order of *Nisi Prius* generally gives the arbitrator power to direct judgment (instead of a verdict) to be entered, and upon this judgment is signed, without any certificate from the associate. In fact, in this, as in all other judgments on award, the order of reference is the authority for the judgment, and unless this is explicit, no judgment can be signed.

The Form in this and the last preceding case will be No. 28.

In all cases the original order, or a duplicate, and the original award must be produced on signing judgment.

CHAPTER XIX.

JUDGMENT BY RULE OF COURT, ON MOTION FOR JUDGMENT, DEMURRER AND SPECIAL CASE.

By Order 40, rule 1, of the Judicature Act, "Except where by the Act or these Rules it is provided that judgment may be obtained in any other manner, the judgment of the Court shall be obtained by motion for judgment."

Judgment in various cases of default and others arising out of the pleadings, having been provided for by rules already cited, judgment by direction of the Judge at or after the trial by Order 36, rule 22a, *post*, and other judgments by the old practice saved by sec. 21, the present Rule will apply to all judgments for which no other authority can be found. Of these the principal would come under the following Rules:—

Order 29, rule 10. In all other actions than those in the preceding Rules of this order mentioned, if the defendant makes default in delivering a defence or demurrer, the plaintiff may set down the action on motion for judgment, and such judgment shall be given as upon the statement of claim the Court shall consider the plaintiff to be entitled to.

Rule 11. Similar as to one of several defendants.

Rule 13. In any case in which issues arise in an action, other than between plaintiff and defendant, if any party to any such issue makes default in delivering any pleading, the opposite party may apply to the Court or a Judge for such judgment, if any, as upon the pleadings he may appear to be entitled to. And the Court may order judgment to be entered accordingly, or may make such other order as may be necessary to do complete justice between the parties.

Order 40, rule 3. Where at the trial of an action the Judge or Referee abstains from directing any judgment to be entered, the plaintiff may set down the action on motion for judgment. If he does not so set it down and give notice thereof to the other parties within ten days after the trial, any defendant may set down the action on motion for judgment, and give notice thereof to the other parties.

Rule 4. Where, at or after the trial of an action by a jury, the Judge has directed that any judgment be entered, any party may, without any leave reserved, apply to set aside such judgment, and enter any other judgment, on the ground that the judgment directed to be entered is wrong by reason of the Judge having caused the finding to be wrongly entered with reference to the finding of the jury upon the question or questions submitted to them.

Where, at or after the trial of an action before a Judge, the Judge has directed that any judgment be entered, any party may, without any leave reserved, apply to set aside such judgment, and to enter any other judgment, upon the ground that, upon the finding as entered, the judgment so directed is wrong.

An application under this Rule shall be to the Court of Appeal.

Rule 11. Any party to an action may at any stage thereof apply to the Court or a Judge for such order as he may, upon any admissions of fact in the pleadings, be entitled to, without waiting for the determination of any other question between the parties. The foregoing Rules of this Order shall not apply to such applications, but any such application may be made by motion so soon as the right of the party applying to the relief claimed has appeared from the pleadings. The Court or a Judge may, on any such application, give such relief, subject to such terms, if any, as such Court or Judge may think fit.

And by sec. 56 of the Act, the report of any official or special Referee "may be adopted wholly or partially by the Court, and may (if so adopted) be enforced as a Judgment by the Court."

These Rules provide for Judgment by Motion

in a great variety of cases, but they are none of them of frequent occurrence. Order 29, rule 10, applies to all actions other than those for a debt or damages, or the recovery of goods or land. Rule 13, to issues with third parties. Order 40, rule 3, to all cases where the Judge has not directed a judgment at or after the Trial. Rule 4 to applications to set aside the judgment directed by the Judge. Rule 11, to admissions of facts in the pleadings, and sec. 56, to references to an official or special Referee. Probably more cases arise under Order 40, rule 4, than under any other rule, as this in fact embraces all appeals from the decision of the Judge at the Trial. The application is made to, and the rule for judgment is entitled in, the Court of Appeal, but it is enforced, and judgment is signed on it, in the same way as on a rule of the Divisional Court. Rule 11 of the same Order introduces a change into the practice; formerly, judgment could have been signed upon any admission of fact in the pleadings, in the same way as by default, but now the Court must be moved to direct a judgment. The most frequent case under this rule is that of a judgment of assets *quando* after a plea of *plene administravit*. In the case of references under sec. 56, it has been decided in *Pontifex* v. *Severn*, 26 W. R. 183, that the official Referee has no power to direct a judgment but can only report to the Court, and judgment must be obtained thereupon by motion.

But besides the cases provided for by these Rules, judgment will always be on Rule of Court on Demurrer (except when it is by default under Order 28, rule 6), and on Special Case, these being matters that must be heard by the Court.

As to the effect of the allowance or overruling of a Demurrer, *vide* Order 28, rules 8, 9, 10, and 11, but the Rule of Court ordering judgment to be entered for the Plaintiff or Defendant on the demurrer is the authority for the judgment.

Under Rule 10, if the Plaintiff demurs to the statement of defence or any pleading of the defendant, and the demurrer is allowed, he will be able to sign judgment on the Rule of Court for whatever he would have recovered by default if the pleading had not been pleaded.

On Special Case the Rule directs judgment to be entered for the Plaintiff or Defendant, and if for the Plaintiff, should state for what amount, and the judgment is signed accordingly.

The Form for all judgments on Rule of Court will be No. 26, and they are to be dated the day they are pronounced: Order 41, rule 2.

CHAPTER XX.

JUDGMENT AFTER TRIAL.

By Order 36, rule 2, Actions shall be tried and heard either before a Judge or Judges, or before a Judge sitting with assessors, or before a Judge and Jury, or before an official or special Referee, with or without assessors. This Rule provides six distinct modes for the trial of an action, but as it has already been shown that judgment cannot be signed on the report of an official or special Referee, it is unnecessary to consider here the result of a trial before them. When the cause has been tried before a Judge, with or without Assessors, or with or without a jury, judgment may be signed in accordance with the directions of the Judge and on production of the associate's certificate, under the following Rules :—

Order 36, rule 22a. Upon the trial of an action, the Judge may, at or after the trial, direct that judgment be entered for any or either party, or adjourn the case for further consideration, or leave any party to move for judgment. No judgment shall be entered after a trial without the order of a Court or Judge.

Rule 23. Upon every trial at the assizes, or at the London and Middlesex sitting of the Queen's Bench, Common Pleas, or Exchequer Division, where the officer present at the trial is not the officer by whom judgments ought to be entered, the associate shall enter all such findings of fact as the Judge may direct to be entered, and the directions, if any, of the Judge as to judgment, and the certificates, if any, granted by the Judge, in a book to be kept for the purpose.

Rule 24. If the Judge shall direct that any judgment be entered for any party absolutely, the certificate of the associate to that effect shall be a sufficient authority to the proper officer to enter judgment accordingly. The certificate may be in the form No. 15 in Appendix (B.) hereto.

And by Order 41, rule 5, already cited, the production of the Certificate shall be a sufficient authority to the officer to enter judgment.

One of the most radical changes effected in the Common Law by the Judicature Act is that brought about by the concluding sentence of Rule 22*a*, "No judgment shall be entered after a trial without the direction of a Court or Judge." By this the verdict of the Jury upon the issues submitted to them at the Trial is rendered inoperative, until it has been directed by the Judge to be carried into effect. Formerly, the successful party was entitled to judgment on the verdict of the jury, fourteen days after the trial. The Judge might expedite or delay judgment and execution, but the *postea* indorsed by the associate on the record setting out the verdict of the Jury was the authority for the judgment, with or without the intervention of the Judge. Now his directions are the sole authority for the judgment, which may be signed immediately on production of the associate's certificate.

The directions of the Judge must be taken from the certificate, and set out *verbatim* in that part of the form of judgment which applies to them, and the operative words of the judgment must follow them as nearly as possible.

The judgment may be for the Plaintiff simply, or for the Defendant simply, or for the Defendant on counterclaim, or for the Plaintiff on some issues and for the Defendant on others, and it may be for or against a third party when one is introduced.

When the judgment is complex, that is, for the Plaintiff on some issues, and for the Defendant on others, either with or without damages, or when a third party has been introduced, and the judgment is either for or against him, the whole of the directions of the Judge must be carried out and embodied in one judgment.

The judgment will be entered against each party affected by it, and each party recovering damages or costs, and entitled to have execution, may take an office copy, which will be of the same force and effect as the original judgment, and upon which he may tax his costs, take his allocatur, and issue execution if necessary.

When the cause has been tried before a Judge and a Jury, it does not necessarily follow that the judgment ordered to be entered by the Judge will exactly correspond with the verdict of the Jury, but the officer of the Court has nothing to do with this, the judgment must be entered exactly as the Judge directs.

By Order 41, rule 6, *ante*, a judgment of Nonsuit now has the same effect as a judgment for the Defendant on the merits, unless otherwise directed by the Court or a Judge. Although no judgment is signed on an order of the Judge or Master at Chambers dismissing the action for want of prosecution, judgment dismissing the action may be signed when the Plaintiff does not appear at the trial, under the following rule:—

Order 36, rule 19. If, when an action is called on for trial, the defendant appears, and the plaintiff does not appear, the defendant, if he has no counterclaim, shall be entitled to judgment dismissing the action, but if he has a counterclaim, then he may prove such claim, so far as the burden of proof lies upon him.

A copy of the pleadings must be filed on signing judgment, whether the judgment is for the Plaintiff or the Defendant, and this is generally the copy which has been already used by the associate and returned by him to the successful party with his certificate; the certificate is merely produced and not filed.

If the judgment is for the Plaintiff, after trial before a Jury, the Form will be No. 29; if for the Defendant, No. 30; if it is after trial before a Judge without a Jury, Form No. 31 can be adapted to either case; in all cases it will be dated the day it is pronounced by the Judge.

Forms can scarcely be prepared to meet the more complicated and unusual cases, but those given will serve as guides as far as they go.

CHAPTER XXI.

JUDGMENT FOR DEFENDANT.

Judgment may be for the Defendant as well as for the Plaintiff on Judge's Order, Master's Certificate, County Court Certificate, Award, Demurrer, Special Case, Rule of Court and after Trial, and these will be found under their several heads.

But there is one Judgment necessarily for the Defendant, and not yet mentioned, viz., on Discontinuance.

By Order 23, rule 1, the Plaintiff may, at any time before the receipt of the defendant's statement of defence, or after the receipt thereof, before taking any other proceeding in the action (save any interlocutory application), by notice in writing, wholly discontinue his action, or withdraw any part or parts of his alleged cause of complaint, and thereupon he shall pay the defendant's costs of the action, or, if the action be not wholly discontinued, the defendant's costs occasioned by the matter so withdrawn. Such costs shall be taxed, and such discontinuance or withdrawal, as the case may be, shall not be a defence to any subsequent action. Save as in this rule otherwise provided, it shall not be competent for the plaintiff to withdraw the record or discontinue the action without leave of the Court or a Judge, but the Court or a Judge may, before, or at, or after the hearing or trial, upon such terms as to costs, and as to any other action, and otherwise as may seem fit, order the action to be discontinued, or any part of the alleged cause of complaint to be struck out. The Court or a Judge may, in like manner, and with the like discretion as to terms upon the application of a defendant, order the whole or any part of his alleged grounds of defence or counter-claim to be withdrawn or struck out, but it shall not be competent to a defendant to withdraw his defence, or any part thereof, without such leave.

Rule 2a. A defendant may sign judgment for the costs of an action, if it is wholly discontinued, or for the costs occasioned by the matter withdrawn, if the action be not wholly discontinued

The only authority necessary for entering judgment under the above rule, is the production of the notice to discontinue, a copy of which should be filed with the pleadings in cases in which there are any.

The Form will be No. 32.

When an order is made dismissing the action for want of prosecution under Order 29, rule 1, no judgment is signed, but the costs may be taxed, and execution issued on the order.

CHAPTER XXII.

NEW AND THIRD PARTIES.

The power of bringing into the action, at any stage of the proceedings, parties not named in the writ, either by direction of the Court or a Judge, or by the service of a mere notice, is a creation of the Judicature Acts, and was utterly unknown to the old practice. Cases of misjoinder or nonjoinder might have been amended by the Court or a Judge, either at or before the Trial; or the Plaintiff might himself have amended his writ after a plea in abatement, but that was all. This plea is now abolished by Order 19, rule 13—"No plea or defence shall be pleaded in abatement"—and as the practice with regard to added parties is entirely new, it may be as well to set out here the principal Rules affecting it.

Order 16, rule 13. No action shall be defeated by reason of the misjoinder of parties, and the Court may in every action deal with the matter in controversy, so far as regards the rights and interests of the parties actually before it. The Court or a Judge may, at any stage of the proceedings, either upon or without the application of either party, and on such terms as may appear to the Court or a Judge to be just, order that the name or names of any party, or parties, whether as plaintiffs or as defendants, improperly joined, be struck out, and that the name or names of any party or parties, whether plaintiffs or defendants, who ought to have been joined, or whose presence before the Court may be necessary in order to enable the Court effectually and completely to adjudicate upon and settle all the questions involved in the action, be added. No person shall be added as a plaintiff suing without a next friend, or as the next friend of a plaintiff under any disability, without his own consent thereto. All parties whose names are so added as defendants, shall be served with a summons or notice in manner hereinafter mentioned, or in such manner as may be prescribed by any special order, and the proceedings against them shall be deemed to have begun only on the service of such summons or notice.

Rule 14. Any application to add or strike out, or substitute a plaintiff or defendant may be made to the Court or a Judge at any time before trial by motion or summons, or at the trial of the action in a summary manner.

Rule 15. Where a defendant is added, unless otherwise ordered by the Court or Judge, the plaintiff shall file an amended copy of and sue out a writ of summons, and serve such new defendant with such writ or notice in lieu of service thereof in the same manner as original defendants are served.

Rule 16. If a statement of claim has been delivered previously to such defendant being added, the same shall, unless otherwise ordered by the Court or Judge, be amended in such manner as the making such new defendant a party shall render desirable, and a copy of such amended statement of claim shall be delivered to such new defendant at the time when he is served with the writ of summons or notice, or afterwards, within four days after his appearance.

Rule 17. Where a defendant is or claims to be entitled to contribution or indemnity, or any other remedy or relief over against any other person, or where from any other cause it appears to the Court or a Judge that a question in the action should be determined not only as between the plaintiff and defendant but as between the plaintiff, defendant, and any other person, or between any or either of them, the Court or a Judge may, on notice being given to such last-mentioned person, make such order as may be proper for having the question so determined.

Rule 18. Where a defendant claims to be entitled to contribution, indemnity, or other remedy or relief over against any person not a party to the action, he may, by leave of the Court or a Judge, issue a notice to that effect, stamped with the seal with which writs of summons are sealed. A copy of such notice shall be filed with the proper officer and served on such person according to the rules relating to the service of writs of summons. The notice shall state the nature and grounds of the claim, and shall, unless otherwise ordered by the Court or a Judge, be served within the time limited for delivering his statement of defence. Such notice may be in the form or to the effect of the Form No. 1 in Appendix (B) (*a*) hereto, with such variations as circumstances may require, and therewith shall be served a copy of the statement of claim, or if there be no statement of claim, then a copy of the writ of summons in the action.

Rule 19. Where under Rule 17 of this Order it is made to appear to the Court or a Judge at any time before or at the trial that a question in the action should be determined, not only as between the plaintiff and defendant, but as between the plaintiff and defendant and any other person, or between any or either of them, the Court or a Judge, before or at the time of making the order for having such question determined, shall direct such notice to be given by the plaintiff at such time and to such person and in such manner as may be thought

---

(*a*) As this form does not warrant a judgment it has not been thought necessary to set it out.

proper, and if made at the trial, the Judge may postpone such trial as he may think fit.

Rule 20. If a person not a party to the action, who is served as mentioned in Rule 18, desires to dispute the plaintiff's claim in the action as against the defendant on whose behalf the notice has been given, he must enter an appearance in the action within eight days from the service of the notice. In default of his so doing, he shall be deemed to admit the validity of the judgment obtained against such defendant, whether obtained by consent or otherwise. Provided always, that a person so served and failing to appear within the said period of eight days may apply to the Court or a Judge for leave to appear; and such leave may be given upon such terms, if any, as the Court or a Judge shall think fit.

Rule 21. If a person not a party to the action served under these rules appears pursuant to the notice, the party giving the notice may apply to the Court or a Judge for directions as to the mode of having the question in the action determined; and the Court or Judge, upon the hearing of such application, may, if it shall appear desirable to do so, give the person so served liberty to defend the action upon such terms as shall seem just, and may direct such pleadings to be delivered, or such amendments in any pleadings to be made, and generally may direct such proceedings to be taken, and give such directions as to the Court or a

Judge shall appear proper for having the question most conveniently determined, and as to the mode and extent in or to which the person so served shall be bound or made liable by the decision of the question.

It will be seen that these Rules apply to two distinct cases: Rules 13, 14, 15, and 16, to that in which a Plaintiff or Defendant is added by order of the Court or a Judge, and thereby becomes a party to the action; Rule 17, *et seq.*, to that in which a third party is brought in by the Defendant, by a notice issued by leave of the Court or a Judge. In the former case, where a Defendant has been added, the new Defendant is to be served with a copy of the amended writ in the same way as an original Defendant, and would, in the same way, be liable to a judgment for default of appearance. If a statement of claim has been delivered, he is to be served with an amended statement, and would be liable to judgment for default of statement of defence.

In the latter case, where a third party is served with a notice under Rule 18, no judgment can be signed; the Defendant obtains no present relief, and the consequence of non-appearance by the third party is defined by Rule 20 to be that he admits the validity of the judgment obtained by the Plaintiff against the Defendant.

Order 22, rule 5. Where a defendant by his defence sets up any counterclaim which raises questions between himself and the plaintiff along with any other person or persons, he shall add to the title of his defence a further title similar to the title in a statement of complaint, setting forth the names of all the persons who, if such counterclaim were to be enforced by cross action, would be defendants to such cross action, and shall deliver his defence to such of them as are parties to the action within the period within which he is required to deliver it to the plaintiff.

Rule 6. Where any such person as in the last preceding Rule mentioned is not a party to the action, he shall be summoned to appear by being served with a copy of the defence, and such service shall be regulated by the same Rules as are hereinbefore contained with respect to the service of a writ of summons; and every defence so served shall be indorsed in the Form No. 4 in Appendix (B) (*a*) hereto, or to the like effect.

Rule 7. Any person not a defendant to the action, who is served with a defence and counter-

(*a*)   Appendix B.   Form 4.

Indorsement on Copy Defence and Counterclaim to be served on Third Party.

"To the within named X. Y."

"Take notice that if you do not appear to the within counterclaim of the within-named C. D. within eight days from the service of this defence and counterclaim upon you, you will be liable to have judgment given against you in your absence."

"Appearances are to be entered at ——."

claim as aforesaid, must appear thereto as if he had been served with a writ of summons to appear in an action.

Rule 8. Any person named in a defence as a party to a counterclaim thereby made may deliver a reply within the time within which he might deliver a defence if it were a statement of claim.

These Rules govern the practice of introducing a third party, conjointly with the Plaintiff, by way of counterclaim. Unfortunately they are not explicit as to what is to be the result of non-appearance by the third party, and the practice under them has not yet been settled.

By Rule 6, any person not a party to the action must be summoned to appear by being served with a copy of the defence, in the same way as with a writ of summons, and on the defence is to be indorsed a notice, the language of which, as to appearance, is almost identical with that of a writ of summons, and would seem to warrant a judgment in case of default; and by Rule 7, he must appear thereto as if he had been served with a writ of summons, but there is no rule expressly providing for a judgment by default of appearance to this notice. It would seem useless to enact that a person must appear in a certain manner to certain process without providing any penalty for his non-appearance, and under these circumstances, the question appears to be, are the Rule directing him to appear and the language of the Notice sufficient to warrant a judgment as in case of non-appearance to a writ of summons, or does the case come under Order 40, rule 1, and must judgment be obtained by moving the Court?

No doubt the practice on this point will very soon be decided; in the meanwhile, a Form of judgment for non-appearance against a third party (No. 33) is given in case it should be required.

If the third party appears, and the cause goes to trial, a judgment will be directed by the Judge either for or against him, and signed, on the associate's certificate, as part of the judgment in the original action. If it should be in his favour he can take an office copy of it for the purpose of enforcing it.

Order 50, rule 4. Where by reason of marriage, death, or bankruptcy, or any other event occurring after the commencement of an action, and causing a change or transmission of interest or liability, or by reason of any person interested coming into existence after the commencement of the action, it becomes necessary or desirable that any person not already a party to the action should be made a party thereto, or that any person already a party thereto should be made a party thereto in another capacity, an order that the proceedings in the action shall be carried on between the continuing parties to the action, and such new party or parties, may be obtained *ex parte* on application to the

Court or a Judge, upon an allegation of such change, or transmission of interest or liability, or of such person interested having come into existence.

Rule 5. An order so obtained shall, unless the Court or Judge shall otherwise direct, be served upon the continuing party or parties to the action, or their solicitors, and also upon each such new party, unless the person making the application be himself the only new party; and the order shall from the time of such service, subject nevertheless to the next two following Rules, be binding on the persons served therewith; and every person served therewith who is not already a party to the action shall be bound to enter an appearance thereto within the same time and in the same manner as if he had been served with a writ of summons.

Rule 6. Where any person who is under no disability, or under no disability other than coverture, or being under any disability other than coverture, but having a guardian *ad litem* in the action, shall be served with such order, such person may apply to the Court or a Judge to discharge or vary such order at any time within twelve days from the service thereof.

Rule 7. Where any person being under any disability other than coverture, and not having had a guardian *ad litem* appointed in the action, is served with any such order, such person may apply to the Court or a Judge to discharge or vary such order at any time within twelve days from the appointment of a guardian or guardians *ad litem* for such party, and until such period of twelve days shall have expired, such order shall have no force or effect as against such last-mentioned person.

These Rules also provide that any person, not already a party, brought into the action under them, shall be served with the order; and by Rule 5 he shall be bound, subject to the two next following Rules, to enter an appearance thereto within the same time, and in the same manner as if he had been served with a Writ of Summons.

The time to appear to a Writ of Summons is within eight days, but by the two next following Rules, any person served with an order shall have twelve days from the service, if he is under no disability, or from the appointment of a guardian, if he is under disability, to apply to discharge or vary the order. Evidently then, no proceedings can be taken on the order until after the expiration of the twelve days and it appears still more doubtful than, under Order 22, whether a judgment for non-appearance can be taken at all.

CHAPTER XXIII.

THE ATTORNEYS' ACT.

The proceedings under this Act remain unaltered. An order having been obtained, on the application either of the solicitor or client, to tax the solicitor's bill and take accounts between them, and the Master's allocatur having been taken on this order, a subsequent order is obtained to be at liberty to sign judgment for the amount found due to either party, and on this judgment is signed.

The Form will be the same (except as to the title of the cause, which will still be "In the matter of A. B. gent. one, &c., agt. C. D.") as an ordinary Judgment or Judge's order, No. 19.

CHAPTER XXIV.

INTERPLEADER.

By Order 1, rule 2, " With respect to interpleader, the procedure and practice now used by Courts of Common Law under the Interpleader Acts, 1 & 2 Will. 4, c. 58, and 23 & 24 Vict. c. 126, shall apply to all actions and all divisions of the High Court of Justice, and the application by a defendant shall be made at any time after being served with a writ of summons and before delivering defence."

The practice was that all Rules, Orders, &c., made under the Act should be entered of record, and this entry had the force and effect of a Judgment upon which execution might issue for any costs ordered to be paid under sec. 7, 1 & 2 Will. 4, c. 58, and sec. 18 of 23 & 24 Vict. c. 126; but now that by Order 42, rule 20, of the Judicature Acts, "Every order of the Court or a Judge, whether in an action, cause, or matter, may be enforced in the same manner as a judgment to the same effect," the entry of record is not necessary for the purpose of issuing execution, which may be issued on the order itself for any sum ordered to be paid.

No judgment is, or ever was, signed on the verdict of the Jury on the feigned issue.

FORM No. 1.

Judgment for Non-appearance for Liquidated Amount.

187 . No. .

In the High Court of Justice,
        Division.

Between   Plaintiff,
              and
                             Defendant.

[*Date*]   187 .

The defendant* not having appeared to the Writ of Summons herein, It is this day adjudged that the Plaintiff recover against the said defendant £   s.   d. and £   costs.

This form applies to all Judgments for non-appearance where the Defendant has not appeared and the claim is for a liquidated amount, whether under Rules 3, 4, or 5 of Order 13, and whether the Judgment is after personal or substituted service.

---

* Or defendants, or the defendant A. B., or the defendants A. B. and C. D., in cases where some defendants have appeared and others have not.

FORM No. 2.

Judgment for Non-appearance for Recovery of Land.

187 . No. .

In the High Court of Justice,
Division.

Between Plaintiff,
and
Defendant.

[*Date*] 187 .

No appearance having been entered* to the Writ of Summons herein, It is this day adjudged that the Plaintiff recover† possession of the land in the said Writ mentioned.

Although these are the words of the form given in the Act, there seems to be no reason why the land or premises recovered should not be described when it is advisable to do so. It will be observed that this form does not provide for costs, and the practice is not to allow any on Judgments for non-appearance for the recovery of land only.

---

* In cases where some defendants have appeared and others have not insert by defendants A. and B.

† Or, against defendants A. and B.

FORM No. 3.

Judgment for Non-appearance for Recovery of Land and Arrears of Rent when specially indorsed.

                                               187 . No. .

In the High Court of Justice,
           Division.
  Between   Plaintiff,
              and
                                      Defendant.

[*Date*]   187 .

No appearance having been entered to the Writ of Summons herein, It is this day adjudged that the Plaintiff recover possession of* the land in the said Writ mentioned, and £   s.   d. arrears of rent and £   costs.

In this case the claim for rent carries costs if the amount exceeds £20.

---

* Or, describe premises.

FORM No. 4.

Interlocutory Judgment for Non-appearance when a claim for mesne profits, arrears of rent, or damages for breach of contract has been indorsed on a writ for the recovery of land.

                                                  187 . No. .

In the High Court of Justice,
                Division.
   Between   Plaintiff,
                    and
                                       Defendant.

[*Date*]   187 .

No appearance having been entered to the Writ of Summons herein, It is this day adjudged that the Plaintiff recover against the Defendant damages to be assessed.

This judgment should be signed at the same time as the final Judgment for the recovery of the land, as it is grounded on the same documents, *i.e.*, the affidavit of service and certificate of non-appearance.

FORM No. 5.

Interlocutory Judgment for Non-appearance for unliquidated damages. Order 13, rule 6.

187 . No. .

In the High Court of Justice,
    Division.

Between   Plaintiff,
    and
           Defendant.

[*Date*] 187 .

The Defendant not having appeared to the Writ of Summons herein, It is this day adjudged that the Plaintiff recover against the said defendant damages to be assessed.

FORM No. 6.

Judgment for Non-appearance where the defendant has appeared, and the appearance has been struck out by order.

187 . No.

In the High Court of Justice,
        Division.

    Between   Plaintiff,
                  and
                                   Defendant

[*Date*]   187 .

The defendant's appearance herein having been struck out pursuant to the order of   , dated   , It is this day adjudged that the Plaintiff recover against the said defendant £   s.   d. and £   costs.

FORM No. 7.

Judgment under Order 14, rule 1, without conditions.

                                      187 . No. .

In the High Court of Justice,
          Division.

Between   Plaintiff,

                and

                                    Defendant.

[*Date*]   187 .

    The Plaintiff having obtained a Master's order under Order 14, Rule 1, of the Judicature Acts, to be at liberty to sign judgment for* the amount indorsed on the Writ of Summons with interest, if any, It is this day adjudged that the said Plaintiff recover against the defendant £   s.   d. and £   costs.

---

    * Or instead, insert amount if given in the order.

FORM No. 8.

Judgment under Order 14, rule 1, with Conditions.

No. . 187 .

In the High Court of Justice,
           Division.
Between   Plaintiff,
          and
                             Defendant.

[*Date*]   187 .

The Plaintiff having obtained a Master's order made under Order 14, rule 1 of the Judicature Acts, dated   to be at liberty to sign Judgment for   unless   and default having been made, It is this day adjudged that the said Plaintiff recover against the defendant £   and £   costs.

If the conditions are complex, the form of Judgment under Judge's order will be more easily adapted.

FORM No. 9.

Final Judgment for Default of Statement of Defence, for a liquidated amount, or possession of land, when a statement of claim or notice in lieu thereof has been delivered.

187 . No.

In the High Court of Justice,
  Division.

Between   Plaintiff,
            and
                                Defendant.

[*Date*]   187 .

The Defendant* not having delivered any statement of defence, It is this day adjudged that the Plaintiff recover against the said defendant £†   s.   d. and £   costs.

---

* When the judgment is against one or more of several defendants, insert the name or names
† Or possession of the land in the Writ of Summons mentioned.

FORM No. 10.

Interlocutory Judgment for Default of Statement of Defence.

                                            187 . No. .

In the High Court of Justice,
                Division.

Between   Plaintiff.
                  and
                                         Defendant.

[*Date*]   187 .

The defendant not having delivered any statement of defence, It is this day adjudged that the Plaintiff recover against the said defendant damages to be assessed.

FORM No. 11.

Final Judgment for Default of Statement of Defence where the defendant does not require a statement of claim.

          187 . No.

In the High Court of Justice,
    Division.
 Between   Plaintiff,
     and
          Defendant.

[*Date*]   187 .

 The defendant having appeared to the Writ of Summons herein, and stated that he did not require a statement of claim, and not having delivered a statement of defence, It is this day adjudged that the Plaintiff recover against the said defendant £ s. d. and £ costs.

FORM No. 12.

Final Judgment for Default of Statement of Defence under Order 22, rule 3.

187 . No. .

In the High Court of Justice,
Division.

Between   Plaintiff,
         and
                                           Defendant.

[*Date*]   187 .

The defendant having obtained leave to defend under Order 14, rule 1, and not having delivered a statement of defence pursuant to Order 22, rule 3, It is this day adjudged that the Plaintiff recover against the said defendant £   s.   d. and £   costs.

FORM No. 13.

Judgment for Default of Defence where the Statement of Defence is struck out by order.

          187 . No. .

In the High Court of Justice,
    Division.
 Between   Plaintiff,
     and
            Defendant.

[*Date*]   187 .

The defendant's statement of defence herein having been struck out pursuant to the order of   dated   , It is this day adjudged that the Plaintiff recover against the said Defendant

---

 This Judgment may be final or interlocutory, according to the nature of the claim. In the former case add the amount of the debt and £   costs. In the latter, damages to be assessed.

FORM No. 14.

Judgment when the Statement of Defence is struck out for non-performance of certain conditions in a Judge's order.

                                        187 . No. .

In the High Court of Justice,
        Division.

Between '   Plaintiff,
        and
                Defendant.

[*Date*]   187 .

The defendant not having
pursuant to the order of
dated   whereby it was
ordered that unless
the statement of defence should be struck out, It is this day adjudged that the Plaintiff recover against the said defendant

---

This Judgment may be final or interlocutory, according to the nature of the claim. In the former case add the amount of the debt and £ costs. In the latter, damages to be assessed.

FORM No. 15.

Judgment on Confession of Defence.

                                    187 . No.

In the High Court of Justice,
          Division.

   Between   Plaintiff,
                and
                                  Defendant.

[*Date*]   187 .

The Plaintiff having confessed the defence stated in the   paragraph of the defendant's statement of defence, It is this day adjudged that the said Plaintiff recover against the said defendant £   for his costs.

FORM No. 16.

Judgment for not entering Demurrer for argument, under Order 28, Rule 6—For Plaintiff.

             187 . No. .

In the High Court of Justice,
     Division.
  Between   Plaintiff,
      and
            Defendant.

[*Date*]   187 .

  The Plaintiff having, on the   day of delivered a demurrer to the defendant's and the defendant not having entered the demurrer for argument, or served an order for leave to amend, It is this day adjudged that the said Plaintiff recover against the said defendant   and £   costs.

FORM No. 17.

Judgment for not entering Demurrer for argument, under Order 28, Rule 6—For Defendant.

         187 . No. .

In the High Court of Justice,
    Division.
 Between   Plaintiff,
     and
           Defendant.

[*Date*]   187 .

 The Defendant having, on the   day of
delivered a demurrer to the Plaintiff's
and the said Plaintiff not having entered the demurrer for argument, or served an order for leave to amend, It is this day adjudged that the said defendant recover against the said plaintiff £ for his costs.

FORM No. 18.

Judgment for Costs, on taking Money out of Court.

187 . No. .

In the High Court of Justice,
    Division.
 Between   Plaintiff,
    and
          Defendant.

[*Date*]   187 .

 The Defendant having paid into Court the sum of £ and the Plaintiff having accepted the said sum in satisfaction of his entire cause of action, and having taxed his costs at the sum of , and the defendant not having paid the said costs within forty-eight hours, It is this day adjudged that the said Plaintiff recover against the said defendant £ for his costs.

FORM No. 19.

Judgment on Judge's or Master's Order.

          187 . No. .

In the High Court of Justice,
    Division.
 Between   Plaintiff,
     and
           Defendant.

[*Date*]   187 .
 Pursuant to the order of   dated
      whereby it was ordered that

*It is this day adjudged that the
recover against the   £   s.   d.
and £   costs.

---

 * If there are conditions in the order which have not been complied with, insert here, "and default having been made."

FORM No. 20.

Judgment on Warrant of Attorney.

187 . No.

In the High Court of Justice,
    Division.
 Between   Plaintiff,
    and
           Defendant.

[*Date*]   187 .

The defendant having executed a Warrant of Attorney to suffer a Judgment to be forthwith entered up against him for £ and costs of suit, It is this day adjudged that the Plaintiff recover against the said Defendant.

 £   and £3 10s. costs.

FORM No. 21.

Judgment by Confession for recovery of Land.

187 . No. .

In the High Court of Justice,
    Division.

Between   Plaintiff,
              and
                                       Defendant.

[*Date*]   187 .

The defendant   having appeared to the Writ of Summons herein,* and having given notice that he confesses this action as to

It is this day adjudged that the Plaintiff recover against the said Defendant possession of
                    and £   costs.

---

* Where the defendant is not named in the Writ of Summons, but has obtained leave to appear, " pursuant to the order of   dated   ."

FORM No. 22.

Judgment on Master's Certificate, under 17 & 18 Vict. c. 125, s. 3 (Common Law Procedure Act, 1854).

187 .   No.

In the High Court of Justice,
                Division.
    Between   Plaintiff,
                    and
                                        Defendant.

[*Date*]   187 .

This cause having been referred to the Certificate of one of the Masters of this Court under 17 & 18 Vict. c. 125, s. 3, and Master
having certified
and the   having obtained an order to be at liberty to sign Judgment on the said Certificate, It is adjudged that the
recover against the   £   s.   d.
and £   costs.

FORM No. 23.

Judgment on Master's Certificate, under 15 & 16 Vict. c. 76, s. 94 (Common Law Procedure Act, 1852).

                                           187 . No.

In the High Court of Justice,
            Division.

Between   Plaintiff,
            and
                                           Defendant.

[*Date*]   187 .

The Defendant not having * appeared to the Writ of Summons herein, and it having been referred to one of the Masters of this Court to ascertain for what amount Judgment may be signed in this action under 15 & 16 Vict. c. 76, s. 94, and Master   having certified

It is this day adjudged that the Plaintiff recover against the said defendant £   s.   d. and £   costs.

---

* Or, not having delivered a statement of defence.

FORM No. 24.

Judgment on Writ of Inquiry.

187 . No. .

In the High Court of Justice,
        Division.
  Between   Plaintiff,
                       and
                                         Defendant.

[*Date*]   187 .

  The Defendant not having* appeared to the Writ of Summons herein, and a Writ of Inquiry dated   having been issued directed to the Sheriff of   to assess the damages which the Plaintiff was entitled to recover, and the said Sheriff having by his return dated   returned that the said damages have been assessed at £   It is adjudged that the said Plaintiff recover against the said Defendant £   and £   costs.

---

    * Or, not having delivered a statement of defence.

FORM No. 25.

Judgment on County Court Certificate.

187 . No. .

In the High Court of Justice,
Division.

Between Plaintiff,
and
Defendant.

[*Date*] 187 .

This action having been ordered by
under section 26 of 19 & 20 Vict. c. 108, to be
tried in the County Court of
and the Registrar of the said Court having certified
that the result was
It is adjudged that the recover
against the £ , and
£ costs.

FORM No. 26.

Judgment on Rule of Court.

            187 . No. .

In the High Court of Justice,
    Division.
 Between   Plaintiff,
     and
            Defendant.

Dated   187 .
Entered   187 .
 Pursuant to the Rule of * Court herein dated
        whereby it was ordered
.
.

It is this day adjudged that the
recover against the

---

* Or. "of the Court of Appeal."

FORM No. 27.

Judgment on Award when the Action is referred by Order before Trial.

. 187 . No. .

In the High Court of Justice,
        Division.
  Between   Plaintiff,
                and
                                  Defendant.

[*Date*]   187 .

The action having been referred by order of   dated   to the arbitration of   with power to the successful party to sign judgment on the award, unless restrained by any Rule of Court or order of a Judge, and the said   having by his award dated   found
.

and no Rule of Court or Judge's order having been made to set the award aside, It is this day adjudged that the   recover against the   £   and £   costs.

FORM No. 28.

Judgment on Award when the Action is referred at Nisi Prius.

187 .   No. .

In the High Court of Justice,
        Division.

Between   Plaintiff,
              and
                               Defendant.

[*Date*]   187 .

The action having on the   come on for trial before   and a Jury of the   of   and it having been ordered by the Court that* the Jury find a verdict for the Plaintiff subject to the award of   with power to the arbitrator to direct a judgment. And the said   having ordered that Judgment be entered for the   for £   , It is this day adjudged that the   recover against the   £   and £   costs.

---

* When no verdict is taken substitute "the cause be referred."

FORM No. 29.

Judgment for Plaintiff after Trial by a Jury.

          187 . No. .

In the High Court of Justice,
    Division.
 Between   Plaintiff,
     and
            Defendant.

Dated   187 .
Entered   187 .

 The action having on the
been tried before   and
a   Jury of the   of
    , and the Jury having found a
verdict for the Plaintiff for   .
And the said   having ordered
that Judgment be entered for the Plaintiff for
    . Therefore, it is adjudged
that the Plaintiff recover against the defendant
     , and £   for his
costs of suit.

FORM No. 30.

Judgment for Defendant after Trial by a Jury.

            187 . No.

In the High Court of Justice,
    Division.
 Between   Plaintiff,
     and
             Defendant.

Dated   187 .
Entered   187 .

 The action having on the   been tried before   , and a   Jury of the   of   , and the Jury having found a verdict for the defendant   . And the said   having ordered that Judgment be entered for the defendant for   . Therefore, it is adjudged that the Plaintiff recover nothing against the defendant. And that the defendant recover against the Plaintiff £*   , and £   for his costs of defence.

---

 * If the Judgment is for costs only omit.

FORM No. 31.

Judgment after Trial by a Judge without a Jury.

187 . No. .

In the High Court of Justice,
Division.

Between   Plaintiff,
               and
                                             Defendant.

Dated   187 .
Entered   187 .

The action having on the been tried before   , and the said   having ordered that Judgment be entered for the* Plaintiff for   . Therefore, it is adjudged that the Plaintiff recover against the defendant £   , and £   for his costs of suit.

N.B.—Form No. 4 in Appendix (D) to the Judicature Acts, is not applicable to the Common Law Divisions.

If the Judgment is for the defendant, adapt Form 30

FORM No. 32.

Judgment on discontinuance for Defendant's costs.

187 . No. .

In the High Court of Justice,
Division.

Between   Plaintiff,
           and
                                          Defendant.

[*Date*]   187 .

The Plaintiff having given notice in writing that he * wholly discontinues his action, It is this day adjudged that the defendant recover against the said Plaintiff £   for his costs.

---

* Or, withdraws part of his claim.

FORM No. 33.

Judgment for non-appearance against a party added by Counterclaim, under Order 22, Rules 6 and 7.

                                    187 . No. .

In the High Court of Justice,
        Division.

    Between A. B. . . Plaintiff,
        and
        C. D. . . . Defendant.
        and
    Between C. D. . . Plaintiff,
        and
        A. B. and E. F. . Defendants,
                        by counterclaim.

[*Date*]   187 .

    E. F. having been served with a copy of the defence and counterclaim of C. D., the defendant in this action, and not having appeared thereto pursuant to Order 22, rule 7, of the Judicature Acts, It is this day adjudged that the said C. D. recover against the said E. F. £   , and £ costs.

INDEX.

ABATEMENT,
    plea in, abolished, 86

ACTION FOR RECOVERY OF LAND,
    what claims may be joined in, 32
    service of writ on defendant, 33
    service in vacant possession, 20
    not sufficient to sign judgment, 20, 33
    judgment for non-appearance in, 32
    form of judgment for land alone, 100
            for land and arrears of rent, 101
            for mesne profits and damages, 102
    judgment for default of defence, 47
        form of, for land, 107
        for damages, 108
    confession by defendant, 60
        judgment on, 60
        form, 119

ADDRESS
    of deponent to affidavit, 12

AFFIDAVIT OF SERVICE OF WRIT,
    must be filed before proceeding on default of appearance, 10

AFFIDAVIT OF SERVICE OF WRIT (*continued*).
    title, 11
    deponent's address and description, 12
    contents, 13.
    jurat, and before whom sworn, 21

AFFIDAVIT UNDER JUDGMENTS EXTENSION ACT, 5.

AGENT, PLAINTIFF'S,
    affidavit must not be sworn before, 22

AMEND, ORDER TO,
    service of, on demurrer, 51.

AMENDMENT
    of judgment not allowed without order, 3
    of writ, 87.
    of statement of claim, 88

APPEAL,
    judgment on, 76, 77

APPEARANCE. *Vide* JUDGMENT.
    judgment by default of, 7—39
        by third party, to counterclaim, 92
        by new party, under order, 50, rule 5, 95

ARGUMENT,
    not entering demurrer for, 51

ARBITRATOR,
    reference to, 63, 70

ASSESSORS,
    at trial, 79

ASSOCIATE'S CERTIFICATE,
    judgment may be signed on, 80

INDEX.

ATTORNEY, PLAINTIFF'S
    affidavit must not be sworn before, 22

ATTORNEYS' ACT,
    judgment under, 97

AWARD,
    judgment on, 70
        forms, 125, 126

BILL OF EXCHANGE,
    several parties to, may be joined in an action under Judicature Act, 36

BILLS OF EXCHANGE ACT,
    judgment for non-appearance under, 35
    procedure unaltered, 35
    order 9, rule 6, does not apply to, 18, 37

CASE. *See* SPECIAL.

CERTIFICATE,
    of non-appearance required on signing judgment, 4, 8
    associate's, judgment on, 80
    master's,   ,,   62, 64
    of registrar of County Court, 68
    of judgment, 5
        under Judgments Extension Act, 5

COMMISSIONER,
    affidavit sworn before. *Vide* AFFIDAVIT.

COMMON LAW PROCEDURE ACT, 1852,
    applies to proceedings under Bills of Exchange Act, 38
    reference to master under, 64
        to arbitrator, 71

COMMON LAW PROCEDURE ACT, 1854
reference to master under, 62

COMPANY,
service of writ on, 19

CONFESSION,
of defence, judgment on, 53
of action for land, judgment on, 60

CONSENT,
order by. *Vide* ORDER.

CONTRIBUTION
from third party, 88

CORPORATION,
service of writ on, 18

COSTS,
on judgment for non-appearance, 4

COUNTERCLAIM,
against third party, 91
service of, 92
appearance to, 92

COUNTY COURT,
issue may be sent for trial in, 68
judgment on certificate of registrar of, 69

COURT, RULE OF,
judgment on, 74

COURT OF APPEAL,
application to, 76

INDEX.

DAMAGES,
    assessment of, 30, 46
    claim for, in addition to recovery of land, 32
    interlocutory judgment for, 48

DATE,
    of judgment, 4

DEFAULT,
    of appearance, 7—39
    of defence, 43—50

DEFENDANT,
    judgment for, 84

DEMURRER,
    judgment on, 78
        for not entering, 51

DISCONTINUANCE,
    by plaintiff by notice, 84
    judgment for defendant on, 85

DISMISSAL OF ACTION,
    by order, 85
    at the trial, 82

EJECTMENT. *See* ACTION FOR RECOVERY OF LAND.

ENTRY OF DEMURRER FOR ARGUMENT, 51

ENTRY OF JUDGMENT, 1—6

EXECUTION, 6

FEES,
    on signing judgment, 5
    filing affidavit, 5
    taking office copy, 5
    searching, 6

FILING
    affidavit of service, 3, 10, 27
    order to proceed, 3
    pleadings, 1

FORMS.
    judgment for non-appearance for liquidated amount, 99
                 recovery of land, 100
                        arrears of rent, 101
        interlocutory for mesne profits, &c., 102
                  damages, 103
    where appearance struck out, 104
    under Order 14, rule 1
        without conditions, 105
        with conditions, 106
        for default of statement of defence, final, 107
            interlocutory, 108
            default of statement of defence, where statement of claim not required, 109
    under Order 22, rule 3,...110
    where statement of defence struck out by order, 111, 112
    on confession of defence, 113
    for not entering demurrer for argument—
        for plaintiff, 114
            defendant, 115
    for costs on taking money out of Court, 116
    on judge's order, 117
        warrant of attorney, 118
    by confession for recovery of land, 119
    on master's certificate, 120
    Common Law Procedure Act, 1854, 120
                                   1852, 121
    on writ of inquiry, 122
    County Court certificate, 123
    rule of court, 124
    award referred before trial, 125
        at *nisi prius*, 126
    after trial by a jury,
            for plaintiff, 127
            for defendant, 128
    after trial without jury, 129

FORMS *(continued).*
> judgment for defendant on discontinuance, 130
>> against third party for non-appearance, 131

GUARDIAN,
> appointment of, 16, 95

HUSBAND AND WIFE,
> service of writ on, 15

INDORSEMENT OF WRIT,
> special under Order 3, rule 6,...7, 8, 9, 41
> under Order 13, r. 5,...28
>> r. 6,...30
>> rr. 7, 8,...32
> of service, 14

INFANT,
> service of writ on, 15
> default of appearance by, 16

INTEREST,
> must be claimed on writ, 10

INTERLOCUTORY JUDGMENT, 30, 34, 48
> forms, 103, 108

INTERPLEADER, 98

JUDGE,
> trial before, 79
> must direct judgment, 80

JUDGE'S ORDER,
> judgment on, 58

JUDGMENT,
    on non-appearance,
        after personal service of specially indorsed writ, 7—25
        substituted service, 26
        where writ not specially indorsed, 28
        form, 99
        where claim unliquidated, 30
        form, 103
        for recovery of land, land and mesne profits, and damages, 32—34
        forms, 100, 101, 102
        under Bills of Exchange Act, 35—38
  where the appearance is struck out by order, 39
  forms, 104, 117
  under Order 14, rule 1,...40
        forms, 105, 106
  for want of statement of defence, 43—50
        forms, 107—112
  for not entering demurrer for argument, 51
        forms, 114, 115
  on confession of defence, 53
        form, 113
  on taking money out of Court, 55
        form, 116
  on judge's order, 58
        form, 117
  on warrant of attorney and cognovit, 60
        forms, 118, 119
  on master's certificate, 62—66
        forms, 120, 121
  on writ of inquiry, 67
        form, 122
  on County Court certificate, 68
        form, 123
  on award, 70—73
        forms, 125, 126
  on rule of Court, 74—78
        form, 124
  after trial, 79—83
        forms, 127, 128, 129
  for defendant, 84
        form, 130

JUDGMENT (*continued*).
    against third party, 93
        form, 131
    under Attorneys' Act, 97
        form, 117

JUDGMENT, ENTRY OF, 1—6

JUDICATURE ACTS,
    orders and rules of. *Vide* ORDERS.

JURY,
    trial before, 79

LAND,
    action for recovery of. *Vide* ACTION.

LUNATIC,
    service on, 15
    default of appearance by, 16

MARRIED WOMAN,
    service on, 15

MOTION FOR JUDGMENT,
    judgment on, 74

MASTER'S CERTIFICATE,
    judgment on, 62

MASTER'S ORDER. *See* JUDGE'S ORDER.

NEW AND THIRD PARTIES, 86—96

NONSUIT, 2, 82

INDEX.

NON-APPEARANCE,
 judgment on, 7—39. *See* JUDGMENT.

NOTICE,
 of entry of demurrer for argument, 51
 of confession in action for recovery of land, 60
 in lieu of statement of claim, 44

ORDERS AND RULES OF THE JUDICATURE ACTS.
 Order 1, rule 2,...98
 ,, 2, ,, 6,...35
 ,, 3, ,, 6,...8
 ,, 9, ,, 2,...26
 ,, ,, 3,...15
 ,, ,, 4,... ,,
 ,, ,, 5,... ,,
 ,, ,, 6,...16
 ,, ,, 6a,..17
 ,, ,, 7,...18
 ,, ,, 8,...20
 ,, ,, 13,...14
 ,, 10 ,...26
 ,, 11 ,, 5,...25
 ,, 13 ,, 1,...16
 ,, ,, 2,...10
 ,, ,, 3,...8
 ,, ,, 4,...21
 ,, ,, 5,...28
 ,, ,, 6,...30
 ,, ,, 7,...32
 ,, ,, 8,... ,,
 ,, 14 ,, 1,...40
 ,, 16 ,, 5,...36
 ,, ,, 13,...86
 ,, ,, 14,...87
 ,, ,, 15,... ,,
 ,, ,, 16,...88
 ,, ,, 17,.. ,,
 ,, ,, 18,... ,,
 ,, ,, 19,...89
 ,, ,, 20,...90
 ,, ,, 21,... ,,
 ,, 19, ,, 2,...43
 ,, 20, ,, 3,...53

ORDERS AND RULES OF THE JUDICATURE ACTS (*continued.*)

Order 21, rule 4,...44
,,   22, ,,   1,...45
,,   ,,   2,... ,,
,,   ,,   3,... ,,
,,   ,,   5,...91
,,   ,,   6,...92
,,   ,,   7,... ,,
,,   ,,   8,...93
,,   23, ,,   1,...84
,,   ,,   2A...85
,,   28, ,,   6,...51
,,   29, ,,   2,...45
,,   ,,   3,...46
,,   ,,   4,... ,,
,,   ,,   5,... ,,
,,   ,,   6,...47
,,   ,,   7,... ,,
,,   ,,   8,... ,,
,,   ,,   10,...74
,,   ,,   11,...75
,,   ,,   13,... ,,
,,   30, ,,   1,...55
,,   ,,   4,... ,,
,,   36, ,,   2,...79
,,   ,,   22a,... ,,
,,   ,,   23,...80
,,   ,,   24,... ,,
,,   40, ,,   1,...74
,,   ,,   3,...75
,,   ,,   4,... ,,
,,   ,,   11,...76
,,   41, ,,   1,...1
,,   ,,   2,...2
,,   ,,   3,... ,,
,,   ,,   4,... ,,
,,   ,,   5,... ,,
,,   ,,   6,... ,,
,,   50, ,,   4,...94
,,   ,,   5,...95
,,   ,,   6,... ,,
,,   ,,   7,... ,,
,,   57, ,,   2,...14

ORDER, JUDGE'S, OR MASTER'S,
    judgment on, 58

ORDER 14, RULE 1,
    judgment on, 40

PARTICULARS OF CLAIM,
    to be filed when not indorsed on writ, 28

PARTIES,
    new and third, 86—96

PARTNERS,
    sued in name of firm, 16, 17

PAYMENT INTO COURT, 55

REFERENCE,
    to arbitrator, by order at chambers, 70
    at the trial, 72
    to the master under Common Law Procedure Act, 1854, 62
    to the master under Common Law Procedure Act, 1852, 64

REGISTRAR OF COUNTY COURT,
    to certify result of hearing, 68
    judgment on his certificate, 69

RULE OF COURT,
    judgment on, 74

RULES AND ORDERS OF THE JUDICATURE ACT,
    See ORDERS.

INDEX. 145

RULES OF HILARY TERM, 1853
    rule 138,...12
      „ 139,...21
      „ 140,... „
      „ 141,.. „
      „ 142,...22
      „ 143,... „
      „ 144,... „
      „   55,...65, 67
      „ 171,...65

RULE OF MIC. VAC., 1854,...13.

SERVICE OF WRIT OF SUMMONS,
    on defendant personally, 13
    on husband and wife, 15
    on infant, 15
    on lunatic, 16
    on firm, 16
    on corporation, 18
    on company, 19
    in vacant possession, 20
    substituted, 26
    to be indorsed on writ, 14

SPECIAL CASE,
    judgment on, 78

SPECIAL INDORSEMENT,
    on writ of summons, 8, 41

STAMPS,
    fees to be paid in, 5

STATEMENT OF CLAIM, 43
    notice in lieu of, 44

STATEMENT OF DEFENCE,
    judgment by default of, 43—50

TAKING MONEY OUT OF COURT,
   judgment on, 55

THIRD PARTIES, 86–96

TITLE,
   of affidavit, 11
   of counterclaim, 92

TRIAL,
   judgment after, 79

WARRANT OF ATTORNEY,
   judgment on, 60

WRIT OF SUMMONS,
   indorsement of. *See* **INDORSEMENT**.
   service of. *See* **SERVICE**.

THE END.

www.ingramcontent.com/pod-product-compliance
Lightning Source LLC
Chambersburg PA
CBHW030335170426
43202CB00010B/1133